CERVANTES' CHRISTIAN ROMANCE

CERVANTES'
CHRISTIAN ROMANCE

A Study of
Persiles y Sigismunda

ALBAN K. FORCIONE

PRINCETON, NEW JERSEY
PRINCETON UNIVERSITY PRESS
1972

160493

Publication of this book has been aided
by the Whitney Darrow Publication Reserve Fund
of Princeton University Press

This book has been composed in Linotype Granjon
Printed in the United States of America
by Princeton University Press, Princeton, New Jersey

Preface

THIS BOOK is a revised version of the final section of my doctoral dissertation, the main part of which was published in 1970 under the title of the original thesis, *Cervantes, Aristotle, and the "Persiles."* Although *Cervantes' Christian Romance* is an entirely separate and different book, I trust that readers familiar with the earlier work will forgive the inevitable repetition here of certain arguments concerning the relation of the *Persiles* to Renaissance literary theory.

I wish to express my thanks to Professors Vicente Llorens and Raymond S. Willis, who directed the thesis and have continued to offer me guidance and encouragement, and to Professors Robert Hollander, Edmund L. King, and Stephen Gilman for their close readings of the manuscript and their much heeded valuable criticisms and suggestions.

Special thanks are due to Professor Ira O. Wade, who convinced me that the subject of the book merited an independent study and should not be subordinated to the concerns of *Cervantes, Aristotle, and the "Persiles."*

I am also grateful to Polly Hanford for her editorial assistance, to Evan Kimble for the use of his library in Göttingen, where I wrote the final version of the book, and to the Whitney Darrow Publication Reserve Fund of Princeton University Press for a generous subvention.

Princeton, New Jersey   A.K.F.

Contents

Preface   v

Introduction   3

Chapter One · Imitation and Innovation

Heliodorus and the Technique of
Fragmentary Exposition   13

The Recurrent Ritual, Allegory, and
Motif   29

Two Potential Objections   51

Chapter Two · Plot

The Chiaroscuros of the Northern
Adventures   64

Periandro's Recitation   77

The Southern Adventures: Toward a
Tone of Comedy   84

Chapter Three · Episodes

The North   108

The South   123

Conclusion. The Structure of the *Persiles*:
Two Analogies   142

Chapter Four · Literature in the *Quixote* and the
Persiles   149

Epilogue · The Poet's Farewell: Where Life and
Literature Meet   157

Index   165

CERVANTES' CHRISTIAN ROMANCE

Introduction

Heralded by its own author as perhaps the best book ever written in Spanish and announced by Philip III's censor as the most learned and entertaining of Cervantes' works, *Los trabajos de Persiles y Sigismunda* enjoyed an immediate success comparable to that of *Don Quixote*. The years following its posthumous publication in 1617 witnessed ten editions, translations into French, Italian, and English, and imitations in prose fiction and drama. In the eighteenth century new editions, imitations, and translations appeared, and in the early years of the nineteenth century a scholar of the stature of Sismondi could still affirm that many readers considered it to be Cervantes' masterpiece.[1]

The past one hundred years have not been so charitable to the *Persiles*. Following the final disintegration of the neoclassical aesthetic, the triumph of the particular over the typical in literary creation, and the dominance of literary tastes by the novel and the valued concerns associated with it—actuality, society, customs, history, biography, and character—the *Persiles* had little to offer the reading public and was quickly relegated to the shelves of libraries and the arcana of literary historians. Among Cervantists detractors have outnumbered admirers of the work, and even the latter have insisted on viewing it with nineteenth-century literary values in mind, redeeming the second half of the work for its "realism" while scoring the fantastic excesses of the first half. For nearly all of them the *Persiles* has remained a disturbing anomaly, to be dealt with most

[1] See Rudolph Schevill, "Studies in Cervantes: I. 'Persiles y Sigismunda': Introduction," *Modern Philology*, 4 (1906-1907), 1-24.

swiftly and conveniently through biographical generaliza-
tion. Thus the "two Cervantes" of Menéndez y Pelayo, the
one aspiring to the impossible realms of the ideal and the
fantastic—the world of the *Galatea*, the *Persiles*, and the
"idealistic" novella—the other preoccupied with the flow
of real, human experience and possessed of a keen critical
faculty which inexorably cut short his flights into fantasy,
the Cervantes of *Don Quixote* and the "realistic" novella.
Thus the attribution of Cervantes' creation of the *Persiles*
to the undeveloped mental faculties of youth or to the
diminished ones of old age. For Arturo Farinelli, the *Persiles* is the last romantic dream of a weary and serene ge-
nius; for Mack Singleton, it is a clumsy adventure story
composed by a youthful Cervantes, who wisely kept it
well hidden until money was short and death was certain.[2]

Even some of the more historical and analytical approaches to the *Persiles* have not overcome the tendency to
see the work as the creation of a "different" Cervantes.
Cesare De Lollis could acknowledge the greatness of the
Cervantes who, to recall Toffanin's words, "smiled" at the
neo-Aristotelian critical movement, and could go on to
maintain that there was another Cervantes, who fell victim
to literary theories which led to the cult of the marvelous
and the empty mannerism in literature to which the
Italian term *secentismo* commonly refers—the "reactionary
Cervantes" of the *Persiles*. For Hatzfeld the careful con-
sideration of style in *Don Quixote* yielded a similar con-

[2] See Menéndez y Pelayo, "Cultura literaria de Miguel de Cervantes y elaboración del 'Quijote,'" *Discursos* (Madrid, 1956);
Farinelli, "El último sueño romántico de Cervantes," *Ensayos y
discursos de crítica literaria hispano-europea*, Vol. I (Rome, 1925);
Singleton, "El misterio del *Persiles*," *Realidad*, 2 (1947), 237-253.

clusion, a distinction between "dem echten, dem span-
ischen Cervantes, dem Cervantes der Urerlebnisse" and
"dem nachahmenden, dem modischen, dem in fremden
Schulen lernenden Cervantes, dem Cervantes der Bild-
ungserlebnisse," the Cervantes who created the *Persiles*.[3]

It is only in the last twenty-five years that criticism has
begun to take the *Persiles* seriously, to see it in its historical
circumstances rather than in the context of contemporary
literary preferences, and to consider it as an independent
work of art. The exploration of the great impact of neoclassical literary theory on Cervantes, as well as the study
of Renaissance discussions and evaluations of Heliodorus'
Aethiopica, has thrown much light on Cervantes' intentions and aspirations in his final work. We may still agree
with Menéndez y Pelayo that Cervantes' decision to imi-
tate the Greek romance was a lamentable piece of folly, but
we may at least admit that Renaissance critical opinion
considered the work to be an artfully constructed epic in
prose and a model for all who dared to scale the heights
of Parnassus.

At the conclusion of the Canon of Toledo's discourse on
prose fiction, Pero Pérez, the curate, remarks that no
Spanish writer has yet written a book of chivalry with
good judgment and according to "art and rules," and that,
were one to do so, he could make himself "as famous in
prose as the two princes of Greek and Latin poetry are in
verse." The challenge implicit in the character's words was

[3] See De Lollis, *Cervantes Reazionario* (Rome, 1924); Helmut
Hatzfeld, *"Don Quijote" als Wortkunstwerk* (Leipzig, 1927), p.
223. See also Benedetto Croce's review of J. Casalduero's *Sentido y
forma de "Los trabajos de Persiles y Sigismvnda,"* *Quaderni della
Critica*, 12 (1948), 71-78.

taken up by the author, and Cervantes set out to gain admittance to the lofty literary society of the epic poets. He was not alone in his endeavor, and he knew where to look for guidance. The cult of epic poetry and the imitation of its classical exemplars was proclaimed everywhere in Renaissance poetics, and theorists, through the exegesis of Aristotle's *Poetics* and Horace's *Ars Poetica*, developed a large and complex body of literary principles, judgments, and precepts to guide the contemporary writer.

In the writings of the theorists, Cervantes learned that the epic poem must have grandeur, that its proper subject matter is heroic deeds and perfect love, that its characters are larger than those of real life, and that, by disseminating knowledge and moral precepts, it fulfills the lofty civilizing mission which Horace had attributed to poetry. Moreover, he could consider the aesthetic principles of Aristotle's *Poetics*, which in his youth had already been turned into precepts by Renaissance commentators: Poetry is defined by imitation rather than meter. The poet's province is poetic truth rather than historical truth, the typical aspects of human conduct rather than those which are unique. The poet's imitation must be both verisimilar and marvelous. The perfect plot, the soul of the epic imitation, is both unified in its presentation of a single action and varied in its incorporation of subordinate episodes. The historical subject is to be preferred in tragedy and epic, as its acceptance and documentation guarantee both grandeur and verisimilitude; nevertheless, it is conceivable that an invented subject could have both qualities.

Toward the conclusion of the *Persiles* the protagonist witnesses a prophetic celebration of "a poet who would bear the name Torquato Tasso and would sing of the liberation of Jerusalem with a plectrum more heroical and pleasing than that of any poet who has sung before him." Evidently, Cervantes shared the enthusiasm of his age for the Italian poet, and it seems likely that he was influenced by Tasso's treatises on poetry as he reflected on the Aristotelian principles and the literary problems and aims underlying them.[4] In the *Discorsi dell' arte poetica* (1587) and the *Discorsi del poema eroico* (1594), Cervantes found not only a systematic presentation of the neoclassical critical system, but also a preoccupation with the good qualities of the popular modern genre—the romance of chivalry. Here was a theorist who was thoroughly imbued with the neo-Aristotelian doctrines and yet was unorthodox enough to maintain that the classical epic could be revitalized only if it were to incorporate such features of the romances of chivalry as had made them so appealing to the modern audience—variety, marvelous subject matter, and the relative contemporaneity in the events and customs which they depict. In effect, the new epic must be a purification of romance. It is of such a process of purification that the Canon of Toledo speaks as he proclaims the classical theories of literature and offers the formula for Cervantes' own new romance. The Spaniard's debt to Tasso's treatises may go beyond the fundamental neoclassical precepts and the general interest in reconciling epic and romance. Discussing the possibility of a completely fictitious but verisimilar imitation, Tasso makes a suggestion which may well have provided the initial idea for the mysterious arctic setting of the *Persiles* and the marvelous customs which it describes: ". . . in poems com-

[4] For Tasso's prestige in Spanish literary circles, see A. Farinelli, *Italia e Spagna*, 2 vols. (Turin, 1929), II, 237-286.

posed in such a manner one should seek material in Gotia and Norveggia, in Suevia and Islanda, or in the East Indies or in the lands which have been recently discovered beyond the Pillars of Hercules."[5]

Like nearly all other neo-Aristotelians Tasso believed that imitation rather than meter distinguishes poetry from historical and other nonpoetical types of writing, and he discusses such works as Heliodorus' *Aethiopica*, Achilles Tatius' *Clitophon and Leucippe*, and the Spanish prose romances of chivalry as belonging to the same species of poetry as do the *Odyssey* and the *Aeneid*. However, it remained for Alonso López Pinciano, the major Spanish theorist of the Golden Age, to discuss the possibility of a prose epic extensively and to offer Heliodorus' *Aethiopica* as an example of its perfectibility. In 1547 Jacques Amyot, the renowned classical scholar and translator, had introduced his French version of the postclassical Greek romance with the claim that, in its conformity to the classical rules and its presentation of edifying moral examples and instructive pieces of rhetoric, it is vastly superior to the romances of chivalry which were so popular among his contemporaries. In his voluminous and widely read *Poetices libri septem* (1561) Julius Caesar Scaliger went further, discussing Heliodorus' methods of disposition together with those of Virgil and concluding that, although not a heroic poem, the *Aethiopica* must be recognized as a model for anyone who wishes to construct an epic successfully. El Pinciano took the final step in the elevation of Heliodorus. In his *Philosophía antigua poética* (1596) he writes that, since imitation rather than meter is the es-

---

[5] *Discorsi del poema eroico*, ed. L. Poma (Bari, 1964), p. 109.

sence of poetry, the *Aethiopica* certainly is an epic poem
and indeed one of the finest that has ever been written. In
its suspenseful tightening of the knot of complication as
its single action moves toward its final peripeteia and
recognition, it is an example of the perfect execution of
Aristotle's formula for the plot of tragedy. In its *in-medias-
res* beginning and delayed exposition it even surpasses
Virgil's and Homer's epics, for the reader's interest in discovering the events preceding the beginning is kept alive
until the exact midpoint of the work. Although it employs
a historical character, Theagenes, a descendant of Achilles,
it is basically a feigned imitation, the type of work sanctioned by Aristotle in Agathon's *Antheus.* However, its
plot is invented with such verisimilitude that the reader's
credulity is never strained so much that he loses faith in
the possibility of the actions imitated. Moreover, Heliodorus is to be praised for choosing as the setting for his
action a land which the Greeks knew only vaguely, for his
audience would accept the grandeur of the events depicted
although they were not attested by historical documentation and would allow the poet considerable license in the
invention of marvelous subject matter. As for its exem-
plarity and instructive value, the work celebrates in Theagenes and Chariklea the triumph of constant and virtuous
love, it depicts virtue rewarded and vice punished, and it
abounds in valuable *sententiae* and educational discourses
on natural philosophy.[6]

[6] For the influence of Tasso on Cervantes, see G. Toffanin, *La
fine dell'umanesimo* (Turin, 1920), Ch. XV; A. Vilanova, "El
peregrino andante en el 'Persiles' de Cervantes," *Boletín de la Real
Academia de Buenas Letras*, 22 (Barcelona, 1949), 97-159, esp. pp.
140-143; E. C. Riley, *Cervantes's Theory of the Novel* (Oxford,

Guided by Tasso and el Pinciano, Cervantes traced the plan for his masterpiece and revealed it in the Canon of Toledo's discourse on the way to compose the ideal romance: "the web woven of beautiful and variegated threads." The plan is still very much alive in 1613, when, on completing the *Exemplary Novels*, Cervantes speaks of a work in progress, "*Los trabajos de Persiles*, libro que se atreve a competir con Heliodoro," and it is finally realized as the author lies on his deathbed in April, 1616: "*Cisne de su buena vejez casi entre los aprietos de la muerte, cantó este parto de su venerando ingenio.*" The offspring of Cervantes' contact with neoclassicism is a lengthy prose narrative describing the adventures and ordeals of a heroic pair of lovers as they wander from the northern part of the world to Rome.

The relatively recent study of Renaissance literary criticism and the impact of the theorists on Cervantes' literary production has done much to clarify the genesis of the *Persiles* and its author's intentions. It has forced Cervantists to be wary of approaching the prose epic with convenient biographical catch-phrases and with modern preconceptions about what constitutes literary quality, and

---

1962), passim; Carlos Romero, *Introduzione al "Persiles" di Miguel de Cervantes* (Venice, 1968), pp. xx ff., lxxxix ff; A. K. Forcione, *Cervantes, Aristotle, and the "Persiles"* (Princeton, 1970), passim, and "Cervantes, Tasso, and the *Romanzi* Polemic," *Revue de Littérature Comparée*, 44 (1970), 433-443. For the influence of El Pinciano, see W. C. Atkinson, "Cervantes, El Pinciano and the *Novelas ejemplares*," *Hispanic Review*, 16 (1948), 189-208; J.-F. Canavaggio, "Alonso López Pinciano y la estética literaria de Cervantes en el 'Quijote,'" *Anales Cervantinos*, 7 (1958), 13-107; Riley, passim; Romero, pp. xx ff., lxxxix ff.; Forcione, *Cervantes, Aristotle, and the "Persiles,"* passim.

it has enabled them to overcome their feelings of per-
plexity as they consider the great differences between the
Persiles and *Don Quixote*. In doing so, it has overthrown
the major obstacles to an understanding of the *Persiles* and
prepared the way for the more important critical task—the
analysis of the work itself.

One of the traditional judgments of the *Persiles* is that
it lacks unity. In 1804 Bouterwek asserted that the two
halves of the work are irreconcilably different, and the
view of the *Persiles* as a "split" work survives in its most
recent commentators, even in the one study which argues
for its thematic unity, Casalduero's *Sentido y forma de
"Los trabajos de Persiles y Sigismvnda."* Moreover, most
critics find that the *Persiles* is overloaded with actions,
characters, and episodes, and that the resulting confusion
defies any attempts to find coherence. For them the work
can adequately be explained only as a collection of independent stories. William J. Entwistle summarizes this view
aptly: "Cervantes, though he kept enough in hand to
promise a new *Decameron* under the title of *Weeks in the
Garden,* packed a score of short stories and anecdotes into
an envelope of romantic adventure, and thus made his
'great *Persiles.*'"[7]

It is undeniable that the *Persiles* is a difficult book and
that its profusion of event and episode will always trouble
its readers. Following our normal habits in reading, we
attempt to assort the various events of the narration in
chronological patterns and fail to hear the sound of recurrent *Leitmotive* or see the recurrent images which
bind all of them tightly together. The *Persiles* is an excep-

[7] *Cervantes* (Oxford, 1940), p. 172.

11

tionally pure example of a long prose narrative that is meant to be read "auditorially" or "visually," as are the literary genres with which it has much in common, the lyric and the drama. As is often the case with lyric and dramatic poetry, its artistry is difficult to discern at a single reading. However, careful examination of the structure of its multiple "independent" units and their interrelationships reveals a striking coherence and simplicity. The work may indeed be the "sunset" of an artist faltering in old age, as Menéndez y Pelayo suggested, but the horizon is unclouded and the glow is still brilliant.[8]

[8] For an informative summary of recent criticism of the *Persiles,* as well as a discussion of the various problems raised by the work, see Rafael Osuna's "El olvido del 'Persiles,'" *Boletín de la Real Academia Española,* 48 (1968), 55-75. I regret that in the preparation of this study I was unable to take into account Tilbert Diego Stegmann's valuable monograph, *Cervantes' Musterroman "Persiles"* (Hamburg, 1971), which appeared when the present work was already in proof.

CHAPTER ONE

Imitation and Innovation

HELIODORUS AND THE TECHNIQUE OF FRAGMENTARY EXPOSITION

THE *Persiles* "ha de ser o el [libro] más malo o el mejor que en nuestra lengua se haya compuesto, quiero decir de los de entretenimiento; y digo que me arrepiento de haber dicho el *más malo*, porque según la opinión de mis amigos, ha de llegar al estremo de bondad posible."[1] In this judgment we can hear the voice of Cervantes the ironist calmly considering the contiguity of the antithetical possibilities. We can also hear the voice of the writer nervously recognizing that his work is radical in character and that, like all literary innovations, it must face up to the possibility of complete failure. Cervantes' earlier pronouncement concerning his final work is equally ambivalent but much more revealing: "libro que se atreve a competir con Heliodoro, si ya por atrevido no sale con las manos en la cabeza."[2] The author fears that the offspring of his inventiveness, education, and imitation may be deformed. The metaphor has a classical ring, recalling the monstrosity to which Horace likened poems composed haphazardly and perhaps also Aristotle's description of the tragic plot as a body which can be embraced in a single

---

[1] "Dedicatoria" (to Part Two), *Don Quijote de la Mancha*, ed. Martín de Riquer (Barcelona, 1958), II, 534. Subsequent page and volume references are to this edition.

[2] "Prólogo al lector," *Novelas ejemplares*, in the *Obras completas*, ed. A. Valbuena Prat (Madrid, 1956), p. 770.

view. Throughout the sixteenth and seventeenth centuries the analogy was repeated by literary theorists, and it was generally used in reference to the structure or disposition of the plot of epic and tragic poetry. The Spanish neo-Aristotelian Francisco Cascales criticized improperly constructed plots by paraphrasing Horace: "Como sueños de enfermos se describen / Sin que conforme el pie con la cabeza,"[3] and the Italian Giraldi compared the well-composed poem to a body, its subject to the skeleton, its episodes and their arrangement to the members, nerves, and ligaments, and its variety of colors to the soft skin.[4] In voicing his fears, Cervantes is revealing that what he considers most radical in the *Persiles* is its highly complex disposition.

It is probable that Cervantes was attempting in the *Persiles* to resolve an aesthetic difficulty which had troubled him from the beginning of his career as a writer. His continuing concern about the problem of disposition in a work of art is easy to trace. In the prologue to the *Galatea* he admits that there are weaknesses in the construction of the work and asks the reader to excuse them.[5] His judgment of the early work becomes harsher in the first part of the *Quixote*, where he writes that "su libro tiene algo de buena invención; propone algo, y no concluye nada,"[6] alluding undoubtedly to its unfinished state and the maze of incomplete narrative threads in which the reader finds

---

[3] *Tablas poéticas* (Madrid, 1779), p. 39.

[4] *Discorsi intorno al comporre de i romanzi, delle comedie, e delle tragedie, e di altre maniere di poesie* (Venice, 1554), pp. 16-18.

[5] Ed. Juan Bautista Avalle-Arce (Madrid, 1961), I, 8-9.

[6] I, 75.

himself enmeshed at the conclusion of the romance. It is interesting that in the *Viage del Parnaso* Cervantes heaps praise upon himself for his powers of *inventio,* but makes no mention of the second major category of rhetorical writing, *dispositio.*[7]

Concern about criticism (undoubtedly Aristotelian in its orientation) of the episodic structure of the first part of the *Quixote* prompts Cide Hamete's discussion of the episodic "flaws" of the work in Part II and his decision to limit his wandering imagination to the treatment of "un solo sujeto" and to introduce only episodes which are "nacidos de los mesmos sucesos" (II, 848-849). Although Cide Hamete is certainly half-serious in such obvious concessions to Aristotle, Cervantes never employs in Part II the loose manner of inserting an episode which his critics had attacked in the *Curioso impertinente* and the *Capitán cautivo* episodes of Part I.

The concessions which Cide Hamete ironically makes to the Aristotelians on the question of the episode are in the Canon of Toledo's discourse on the romances of chivalry the serious literary principles underlying his theory of unity. Invoking the familiar analogy, he laments that he has never seen a romance "que haga un cuerpo de fábula entero con todos sus miembros, de manera que el medio corresponda al principio, y el fin al principio y al medio" and adds that all have "tantos miembros, que más parece que llevan intención a formar una quimera o un monstruo que a hacer una figura proporcionada" (I, 482). The canon appears to be more concerned with flaws in verisimilitude than with flaws in unity in romances and

[7] See ed. R. Schevill and A. Bonilla (Madrid, 1922), p. 55.

does not go into detail as to exactly how the desired proportion in plot is to be achieved by the writer, a matter which aroused a vast amount of theoretical activity among Cervantes' contemporaries. Nevertheless, his use of the body analogy, his emphasis on structural tightness in the relationship between the beginning, middle, and end of a plot, and his adverse judgment of the boundless variety of the books of chivalry identify his position unmistakably with that of the Aristotelian critics of Ariosto and the other romancers on the question of unity.

Attempting to meet the compositional demands of the neoclassical literary school, Cervantes in the *Persiles* turned to a model which was universally praised for its flawless structure. It is worth considering what Renaissance theorists observed in Heliodorus' narrative methods. The first to comment on them was the French translator of the *Aethiopica*, Jacques Amyot, in 1547:

> . . . la disposition en est singuliere: car il commence au mylieu de son histoire, comme font les Poëtes Heroïques. Ce qui cause de prime face vn grand esbahissement aux lecteurs, & leur engendre vn passionné desir d'entendre le commencement: & toutesfois il les tire si bien par l'ingenieuse liaison de son conte, que l'on n'est point resolu de ce que l'on trouue tout au commencement du primier liure iusques à ce que l'on ayt leu la fin du cinquiesme. Et quand on en est là venu, encore a l'on plus grande enuie de voir la fin, que l'on n'auoit au parauant d'en voir le commencement: De sorte que tousiours l'entendement demeure suspendu, iusques à ce que l'on vienne à la

conclusion, laquelle laisse le lecteur satisfait, de la sorte que le sont ceux, qui à la fin viennent à iouyr d'vn bien ardemment desiré, & longuement atendu.[8]

In his treatment of the rules for epic disposition Julius Caesar Scaliger repeated the familiar demand for the *in-medias-res* beginning while making another, based on Aristotle's discussion of the epic poet's license to incorporate into his work varying but relevant episodes to relieve the hearer of the boredom that the poet would inevitably arouse if he limited himself to the narration of the main plot. The poet must employ interruptions and fragmentations of the major narrative thread for the sake of holding the hearer in suspense and arousing in him *admiratio* through the variety which episodes afford. Scaliger concludes his arguments by invoking Heliodorus' *Aethiopica*: "Quem librum epico Poetae censeo accuratissimè legendum, ac quasi pro optimo exemplari sibi proponendum."[9] Similarly Tasso saw in Heliodorus a master of the elusive technique of fragmentary exposition: "Il lasciar l'auditor sospeso, procedendo dal confuso al distinto ... è arte perpetua di Virgilio; e questa è una de le cagioni che fa piacer tanto Eliodoro." Claiming to have employed the technique many times in this work, Tasso points to the

---

[8] *L'Histoire Aethiopique de Heliodorus* (Paris, 1547), n.p. A Spanish translation of Amyot's preface accompanied the first Spanish translation of Heliodorus' work (1554). It is included in F. López Estrada's edition of the *Aethiopica—Historia etiópica de los amores de Teágenes y Cariclea*, tr. F. de Mena (Madrid, 1954), pp. lxxvii-lxxxiii.

[9] *Poetices libri septem*, ed. A. Buck (Stuttgart-Bad Cannstatt, 1964), p. 144.

17

history of Erminia in the *Liberata*: in the third canto of his poem the reader discovers "alcuna ombra di confusa notizia" about the maiden; "più distinta cognizione se n'ha nel sesto; particolarissima se n'avrà per sue parole nel penultimo canto."[10] It is well to note how Tasso's words on his development of the Erminia narrative thread could be applied to Cervantes' exposition of the history of Periandro-Persiles and Auristela-Sigismunda, which is offered to the reader in shadowy fragments and is fully illuminated only in the final chapter of his work. El Pinciano's poetics presents all of these analyses of Heliodorus' narrative methods and adds something new. The plot of the *Aethiopica* is a perfect example of Aristotle's formula for the plot of tragedy—the complication and the unraveling. The knot of complication is tightened until there seems to be no way of unraveling it. However, the skillful poet leaves a "cabo de donde asir," and at the moment of highest tension the knot is unraveled and the catastrophe or peripeteia occurs, bringing a relaxation of tension. Heliodorus surpasses Virgil in the process of "atar y desatar," for despite its length his work presses toward the final peripeteia, which is accompanied by a most artfully constructed recognition, with ever increasing tension.[11] Implicit in all these judgments of Heliodorus' narrative techniques—the *in-medias-res* construction, the delayed exposition, the fragmentation of the narrative through episodic additions, and the peripeteia and recognition—is the theorists' admiration for

[10] *Le lettere di Torquato Tasso*, ed. C. Guasti (Florence, 1853-1854), I, 77-78.

[11] *Philosophía antigua poética*, ed. A. Carballo Picazo (Madrid, 1953), II, 38-39, 83-86.

coherence, tightness, and, above all, suspense as literary qualities.[12]

A glance at the *Persiles* reveals that Cervantes' major debt to Heliodorus and the theorists who analyzed his methods lies in his use of delayed exposition both through the *in-medias-res* beginning in his introduction of individual narrative threads and in the subsequent fragmentation of their development by the introduction of other threads. The process is visible both in the major line of narration, the adventures of the protagonists, whose identity and motives are not fully disclosed until the final chapters of the work, and in the numerous secondary lines of narration, the episodes.

The episode of Feliciana de la Voz demonstrates the narrative methods of the *Persiles* very well. As the pro-

---

[12] For a discussion of the effect of Heliodorus and Achilles Tatius' technique of withholding information from the reader and occasionally letting him wander into the blind alleys into which the characters within the work stumble, see V. Hefti, *Zur Erzählungstechnik in Heliodors Aethiopica* (Vienna, 1950), pp. 113-117. It should be pointed out that modern criticism has not shared the enthusiasm of the Renaissance in its evaluation of Heliodorus' plot construction. Both E. Rohde (*Der griechische Roman und seine Vorläufer* [Leipzig, 1900], pp. 474-475) and V. Hefti (pp. 7-13, 97, 125) express admiration for its artful qualities but qualify their praise by pointing to various irrelevancies in the work. Both O. Schissel (*Entwicklungsgeschichte des griechischen Romans im Altertum* [Halle, 1913], pp. 50-62) and S. Wolff (*The Greek Romances in Elizabethan Prose Fiction* [New York, 1912]) recognize the superior unity of the *Aethiopica* beside the other Greek romances of antiquity, but they find it to be simply the least episodic work of a genre in which the inclusion of irrelevant thematic matter and loose construction were norms.

tagonists journey through Extremadura, a rider emerges from the darkness, deposits an infant with the group of pilgrims, and disappears. Almost immediately thereafter a disheveled woman staggers into the group and begs for protection and food. Some shepherds of the region hide her in a hollow tree trunk, and on the following morning she reveals that she has given birth to an illegitimate child and is being pursued by her vengeful father and brother. Following the clarification of the preceding events, the narration shifts to another episode, and only after its completion does it return to the persecuted mother. The pilgrims visit the monastery of the Virgin of Guadalupe where, much to their surprise, they witness the climactic moment of Feliciana's ordeals. The avenging brother, the father of the infant, and the populace converge on the mother before the altar of the Virgin, and the moments of danger, reconciliation, and rejoicing quickly follow.

The brief episode separating the first and second appearances of Feliciana is essentially the same in structure. As if in recollection of Tasso's recommendations on episodic integration,[13] Cervantes' narrator introduces the episode as an obstacle in his heroes' path: ". . . nunca los buenos deseos llegan a fin dichoso sin estorbos que los impidan, quiso el cielo que el de este hermoso escuadrón . . . fuese impedido con el estorbo que agora oireis."[14] The

---

[13] Asserting that the variety of a poem depends on its episodes and that an episodic plot must be avoided, Tasso recommends that the poet follow Homer and Virgil in introducing only episodes which contain obstacles or aids to the hero in his quest: "Tutta dunque la varietà del poema nascerà da' mezzi e da gli impedimenti" (*Del poema eroico*, ed. cit., p. 148).

[14] *Los trabajos de Persiles y Sigismunda*, ed. Juan Bautista Avalle-

group of pilgrims is resting beside a brook when a young man transfixed by a sword staggers forth from the foliage and collapses. After discovering a small picture of a woman and some lines of poetry in his possession and assuming that he is a victim of a love intrigue, the startled pilgrims find themselves surrounded by the officers of the *Santa Hermandad*, who arrest them as murderers and throw them into prison. After the protagonists have been threatened with torture and the narrator has used the opportunity for some satirical thrusts at bureaucrats, an innkeeper appears to clarify the death of the young man, Diego de Parraces, and allow the release of the captives. The clarification is barely satisfying; for it reveals merely that a relative of the young man committed the murder. Nothing is said of motive or circumstances. This event illustrates how brief and undeveloped the episodes of the *Persiles* can be, how the process of fragmentary exposition and subsequent clarification is maintained even in the briefest episode, how weak the links binding episode to main plot can be, and how self-conscious the narrator can be in drawing attention to the legitimacy of the links.

In the episodes above, the subsequent clarification follows closely on the introductory fragment, and the curiosity that is occasioned in the reader is quickly satisfied. However, in the introduction of other episodes, Cervantes offers an illumination of the obscure fragments only after much delay. The episode of Augustina Ambrosia begins with the puzzling encounter of the pilgrims with a cart bearing thirteen prisoners to the galleys. In it they observe a despairing young man who has covered his

---

Arce (Madrid, 1969), p. 300. Subsequent page references to the *Persiles* are to this edition.

21

face with axle grease and has determined to die of hunger. The compassionate Constança offers the youth a tin of fruit, and the wanderers continue on their way to Valencia. There they survive an attack by Turks, who pillage and burn a town and assault its church before departing with their plunder and their accomplices, the treacherous local *moriscos*. Following this long episode, the pilgrims journey to Barcelona and on the way meet a beautiful shepherdess, who steps forth from a grove of trees, challenges the company with an enigma concerning love and jealousy, and promptly disappears into the grove.[15] On arriving in Barcelona, they visit the harbor, where unexpectedly a beautiful woman emerges from a group that has just disembarked, approaches Constança, recounts the story of her life, and reveals that she was the "youth" whom Constança had aided on the road to Valencia. A similar case of such delayed clarification occurs in the Isabela Castrucho episode, which is introduced by a description of the maiden's entourage as it passes the pilgrims and the brief comments of one of her servants, who asks them for some water. We learn only that Isabela's father is dead and that her rich uncle is escorting her to Italy, where he intends to marry her against her will. After affording us a brief glimpse of Isabela, the narrative shifts to the thread of Bartolomé's and Luisa's fatal passion, then to the arrival of the pilgrims in Milan, and finally to a discussion of love and jealousy. At this point the fragment concerning the unwilling bride is picked up, as the pilgrims arrive in Lucca and witness the successful deception of the uncle by the young girl and her beloved.

---

[15] Such enigmas appeared frequently in sixteenth-century pastoral literature. See *La Galatea*, ed. cit., II, 241 ff. and Avalle-Arce's notes.

If it is obvious that the fundamental narrative method of the *Persiles* derives from Heliodorus, it is no less obvious that Cervantes employs that method to produce a work of much greater complexity than the *Aethiopica*. It is as if he were testing the limits of the method in full awareness that he was running the risk of seeing his creation disintegrate into chaos. Two of the most radical structural features of the *Persiles,* both the result of the Heliodorean technique of fragmentary exposition and subsequent clarification, could be described as extreme involution and nodes of extreme complication. The work is full of characters' narrations of past events—stories within the story—and such stories are generally fragmented by the continuing development of the main plot. This common feature of the Greek romances is complicated in the *Persiles* as occasionally the reported story contains the report of another character—thus, the story within the story within the story. The outstanding example of this type of involuted construction is in Periandro's recitation at the court of King Policarpo, when his description of his encounters with Sulpicia and King Leopoldio contains their accounts of their misfortunes.

If such involution taxes the patience and the memory of the reader, the nodes of extreme complication push his curiosity toward the limits beyond which it ceases to be pleasurable. Events always follow one another at a very rapid pace in the *Persiles.* When several occur nearly simultaneously and the circumstances leading to them are to be clarified subsequently, we witness a node of extreme complication. The outstanding example is in Book III: a woman falls from a tower, a man struggles with another woman at its top, Periandro ascends the tower to save her, both he and the woman's assailant plunge to the earth below, a group of horsemen appears and attempts to abduct one of the companions of the protagonists, and the youthful Antonio drives them off with his arrows. Nothing in the narration has pointed toward these various occurrences, and it is only in the subsequent chapter, which introduces two separate narrative threads, those of the madman in the tower and the attacking horsemen, that the reader learns the identity and the motivation of the participants in the violent scene.

If Cervantes' development of Heliodorus' techniques in the disposition of the plot suggests a departure from the classical formulas, his use of episodes represents an even more radical attempt at innovation. Aristotle wrote that the properly constructed epic poem observes unity of action while presenting a pleasing variety through episode. The difficulty of reconciling the demands for unity and variety quickly became one of the acute problems of sixteenth-century literary theorizing, particularly as classicists recognized that the unrestrained variety of the loosely constructed *romanzi* was an undeniable source of pleasure.[16] There was a great deal of flexibility and rationalizing in the contemporary discussions of the proper integration and subordination of the episode, but nearly all theorists

[16] Much theoretical energy was devoted to the definition and function of episode and to the limits of the poet's license in his use of episode, particularly in the controversy surrounding Ariosto's *Orlando Furioso* and Tasso's *Gerusalemme liberata*. Cervantes was well aware of the issues at stake in the controversy, and indeed in the second book of the *Persiles* he dramatizes a confrontation between the "ancients" and the "moderns" concerning the proper use of episode (see Forcione, *Cervantes, Aristotle, and the "Persiles,"* Ch. VI).

agreed that the episode should never be of such length and interest as to become independent of the major plot and cause the reader to waver in his anticipation of its conclusion. For example, Faustino Summo, in defending Tasso and attacking Ariosto, writes that an episode must never be allowed "to assume the proportions and the character of an independent plot."[17] Moreover, in his criticism of the episodic variety of Ariosto's *Orlando Furioso*, Filippo Sassetti makes a sophisticated distinction between two kinds of episode. The first introduces unrelated subject matter and destroys the suspense aroused in the reader by the main plot. The second, in its brevity and relevance, heightens the reader's suspense by delaying the conclusion of the main plot, which is never allowed to disappear from the reader's attention.[18]

In the *Persiles* Cervantes constantly offends against both precepts. Many of its episodes are provided by the narrations of characters whom the wandering heroes meet on their journey. Like the persons encountered by Theagenes and Chariklea in the *Aethiopica*, they join the heroes' band and occasionally participate in the main plot. Thus the elder Antonio saves the pilgrims from the fire that ravages the island of the barbarians, joins their pilgrimage, and

[17] Cited by Bernard Weinberg, *A History of Literary Criticism in the Italian Renaissance* (Chicago, 1961), II, 1070.

[18] Weinberg, p. 975. The irrelevant episode leads to "il raffreddamento dell affetto gia a muouersi incominciato; il che non auuiene già in quella sospensione danimo, che procede da mandare in lunga il racconto di alcuna cosa, senza che si entri dallo incominciato in un altro proposito." Minturno makes a similar distinction between interruptions which heighten the reader's attention to the movement of the main plot and independent episodes, which distract his attention (see *L'arte poetica* [Venice, 1564], p. 35).

much later involves them in the series of events surrounding his return to Spain: the recognition by his parents, the
death of the count, and the marriage of his daughter.
However, Antonio's extended narration in the cave shel-
tering the protagonists from the fire has nothing to do
with the illumination of the backgrounds of the major
plot and assumes an independence which absorbs the
reader's attention and distracts him from the mysteries
surrounding Periandro and Auristela.

Most of the incidents involving the secondary characters
of the *Persiles* follow the pattern of episodic integration
which we observe here. The narration of their life stories
either precedes or follows their participation in some
events that occur in the quest of the heroes. The degree to
which their narrations are independent and eclipse the
main plot varies. In Mauricio's account of the misfortunes
of his daughter Transila and in Clodio's relation of his
career as a satirist, there is virtually no connection to the
main plot. On the other hand Feliciana de la Voz's narration clarifies an action into which the protagonists have
been drawn, as does the story of the "flying woman,"
which follows Periandro's struggle with the madman atop
the tower.

If the narrative threads of these figures and the protagonists are indeed interwoven with some attention
to the necessity of fusing episode and major plot, the bonds
which Cervantes employs in this task are often very weak
and occasionally disappear altogether. While the wanderers enjoy a brief respite on the Island of the Hermits,
Renato offers them food and lodgings as well as the history
of his life, an independent story with neither direct nor
oblique references that would maintain our interest in or

clarify the main plot. If he had cared to, Cervantes might have justified the inclusion of Renato's tale by Tasso's formula that episodes must present either "mezzi" or "impedimenti" to the movements of the heroes. In other cases the independence reaches beyond all limits set by contemporary theory, however liberally it might have been interpreted. The protagonists meet a character, who offers them the story of his life and then either disappears or participates in the events of the main plot merely by being present. Such are the narrations of the Italian dancing master Rutilio and the Portuguese victim of love, Manuel de Sosa Coitiño. Another type of episode in which independence is absolute is to be found in various events which the protagonists simply observe by accident. The story of Ruperta's revenge, the interlude of the counterfeit captives, and the festival and marriage of the peasants in Toledo are examples of this type.

In summary, the episodes of the *Persiles* often form independent plots with little relation to the main plot. As the bonds attaching them to the main plot weaken, they distract the reader from its development, destroying the effect of suspense for which Heliodorus' technique of disposition had been praised and which, as Sassetti had maintained, the properly constructed episode should heighten. In their multiplicity, the rapidity that marks their introduction and conclusion, and in the continual interruption and fragmentation of both main plot and episode by more episodes, the *Persiles*, far from achieving the proportion which the Canon of Toledo had demanded in the unified variety of the tightly constructed plot, produces rather an effect of confusion, presenting a maze of narrative fragments through which a bewildered reader

27

must make his way. To recall the canon's metaphor, we cannot escape the conclusion that the weave of the *Persiles* is too intricate or, to borrow from Campanella's criticism of Ariosto's dispositional techniques, that Cervantes is "a weaver of wool, linen, and silk, and broom, and thread of gold,"[19] who must cut his cloth and threads so frequently that the result strikes the eye as more akin to a patchwork quilt than to a "tapestry woven of varied and beautiful threads." Over the years readers of the *Persiles* have called attention to its flaws in construction, from the seventeenth-century French translator, le Sieur D'Audiguier, who lamented: ". . . que Cervantes quiere hablar de todo y que todo lo confunde, sacando erróneas conclusiones de sus principios . . . ,"[20] to Mayáns y Siscar, who in 1757 cited the *Persiles* as the example of a work in which episode swallows up plot,[21] to E. C. Riley, who recently wrote: "The *Persiles*, I think, is a practical attempt to come to terms with variety by means of a more flexible form, but not a very confident attempt. It is unsuccessful mainly because he [Cervantes] overloads the structure. The attempt to come to terms is in the end little less than a

[19] ". . . [Ariosto] pare un . . . tessitore—come egli disse—di lana, lino e seta e ginestra e fila d'oro: però bisognali spesso e cinque e sei volte tagliar la tela e la fila con disgusto del lettore" (*Poetica*, ed. L. Firpo [Rome, 1944], p. 151; cited by Weinberg, p. 1069).

[20] *Les Travavx de Persiles et de Sigismonde* (Paris, 1618); the passage is cited in Spanish translation by D. Leopoldo Ríus in his *Bibliografía crítica de las obras de Miguel de Cervantes Saavedra* (Madrid, 1895), I, 364.

[21] See Schevill's introduction to *Persiles y Sigismunda*, ed. R. Schevill and A. Bonilla, 2 vols. (Madrid, 1914), I, xliv.

capitulation."[22] Whatever Cervantes might have thought about his final product, the fears he expressed in the prologue to the *Exemplary Novels* certainly proved to be prophetic. It remains to be seen, however, whether the *Persiles* is in fact the monstrosity which its author had feared.

THE RECURRENT RITUAL, ALLEGORY, AND MOTIF

All that has been said of the structure of the *Persiles* up to this point reveals that Cervantes failed to achieve the goal he had theoretically set for himself in planning his final work. While the difficulties in the episodic weave of the work suggest that Cervantes' fears concerning his powers of disposition were justified and that, try as he might, he could not write successfully the type of prose epic envisaged by the Canon of Toledo and contemporary theorists, they do not necessarily prove that there is no aesthetic coherence in the mass of adventures and narrations which form the surface of the work. Riley is undoubtedly right in observing that Cervantes' "literary theory gives no hint of concern with the more recondite species of unity—thematic and symbolic, as opposed to mere formal unity" and "his expressed ideas on the unity of the novel are

[22] *Cervantes's Theory of the Novel*, p. 130. Werner Krauss observes the breakdown of the plot of the *Persiles* into independent parts and judges its structure to be an example of baroque art: "In dieser Präponderanz der Teile gegenüber dem Ganzen liegt eines der wichtigsten Merkmale dessen, was man barocke Kunst oder Literatur nennt. Die Einheit findet hier nur ihre Verwirklichung in einem Aufgebot der mannigfaltigsten Episoden" (*Miguel de Cervantes: Leben und Werk* [Neuwied, 1966], p. 198).

based on current ideas of epic unity."[23] Such ideas may reveal much about Cervantes' intentions in the *Persiles*, but they tell us little concerning his realization, or the intent of the work itself, and they are certainly inadequate criteria of unity if we wish to understand the work. The fact is that the vision which Cervantes embodied in the *Persiles* had a coherence of its own, one which demanded literary techniques of which Cervantes was theoretically unaware and which compelled him to develop or "abuse" the Heliodorean techniques of disposition which he had studied in the *Aethiopica* and the poetic treatises of his time. That is to say, his vision demanded the independent episode, the proliferation of event and episode, and the continuing fragmentation in the development of narrative threads. Regardless of what Cervantes said about his desires to write a prose epic, the unity of texture or theme of the *Persiles* is to be sharply distinguished from the linear unity acclaimed by sixteenth-century theorists in the classical epic.

The *Persiles* is a quest romance in which the heroes must abandon an imperfect society, journey through strange worlds full of menacing forces, and suffer numerous trials and struggles before reaching their destination. Here their sufferings are rewarded with superior wisdom, and they can return to elevate their society to the state of perfection which they themselves embody. The principal narrative line presents a sequence of adventures involving the heroes, each of which in structure and thematic implications repeats the cyclical pattern of the overall quest. Accompanying the major plot are numerous secondary lines of narration, each forming an episode and presenting a quest

[23] Op. cit., p. 130.

of a secondary figure. Each secondary quest represents a miniature analogue of the quest of the heroes, both in its structure and its thematic implications. The major effect of this structure is an accumulation of power in the statement of theme through ritualistic repetition. Moreover, through fragmentary narration Cervantes succeeds in superimposing the episodes on the main plot, creating a richly complex texture and heightening the effect of timelessness that springs from the recurrence of ritual.

The structure of the *Persiles* is animated by the spirit of orthodox Christianity, as the adventures often have biblical overtones, suggesting an analogy between the heroes, God's chosen in search of the Promised Land, and mankind awaiting the advent of the Redeemer and the establishment of the custodian of his Word, the Holy See in Rome, itself to be followed by the New Jerusalem. Thus one can observe in the *Persiles*, in symbolic concentration, the entirety of history as presented by the Christian mythology. One of the most important factors sustaining this level of analogy is the movement of the heroes from their benighted kingdoms at the northern extremities of the world (Tile, the kingdom of Periandro, is in fact described in the work as the "end of the earth" [p. 465]) to the "cabeza del mundo," Rome (p. 441).[24]

At another symbolic level the quest of Periandro and Auristela reenacts the basic myth of Christianity: man in his fallen state must wander in the sublunary world of

[24] The protagonists seek Catholic instruction, as in the northern kingdoms "la verdadera fe católica no está en el punto tan perfecto como se requiere" (p. 432). "Sigismunda . . . había hecho voto de venir a Roma, a enterarse en ella de la fe católica, que en aquellas partes setentrionales andaba algo de quiebra" (p. 467).

31

disorder, suffering in the world of human history, and be reborn through expiation and Christ's mercy. Here too the symbolic implications of the protagonists' journey have an important function, as they move from a realm menaced by war, an oppressive king, and the threat of sterility to the city which traditionally images the Kingdom of the Blessed. Here, at what might be described in the traditional terminology of allegorical exegesis as the "anagogical" level of the *Persiles*, we discover the importance of the motif of "los trabajos,"[25] which the title announces and which becomes a principle of unity, providing a thematic nexus between the many disparate narrative threads which have little coherence in terms of the current neo-Aristotelian criteria. At two points in the work we discover a traditional Christian commonplace: ". . . están nuestras almas siempre en continuo movimiento, y no pueden parar ni sosegar sino en su centro, que es Dios, para quien

[25] Covarrubias' *Tesoro* (1611) offers two meanings of the word. In addition to the most common meaning of the Latin *labor*, English *work* or *task*, the word also had the important secondary meaning of the English *ordeal* or *trial*: ". . . a qualquiera cosa que trae consigo dificultad o necessidad y aflicción de cuerpo o alma llamamos trabajo" (ed. M. de Riquer [Barcelona, 1943], p. 971). Don Quixote claims that he is "valiente, comedido, liberal, bien-criado, generoso . . . paciente, sufridor de *trabajos*, de prisiones . . ." (I, 501). It should be pointed out that the symbolic range of the *Persiles* includes a celebration of Christian ethical values, particularly those of patience, perseverance, and faith in God in adversity. At this "tropological" level of the work the motif of "los trabajos" is of course equally important. For the popularity and significance of the symbol of the pilgrimage in literature of the Counterreformation, see A. Vilanova, "El peregrino andante en el 'Persiles' de Cervantes," *Boletín de la Real Academia de Buenas Letras*, 22 (Barcelona, 1949), 97-159.

fueron criadas" (p. 275 and p. 458). The *Persiles* represents this apparently endless movement of the soul through the "trabajos" of the earthly life, as its multitude of characters must wander about the earth tormented and driven onward by desire for a point of repose: "Todos deseaban, pero a ninguno se le cumplían sus deseos: condición de la naturaleza humana, que puesto que Dios la crió perfecta, nosotros, por nuestra culpa, la hallamos siempre falta, la cual falta siempre la ha de haber mientras no dejáremos de desear" (p. 176). The point of repose continues to elude them until they emerge from darkness and the sea and reach Rome, that point which images Augustine's center of repose, God and the Heavenly City.[26]

[26] The classical statement of the vision of the restlessness of the soul and its state of unfulfilled desire in its estrangement from Eternity is of course St. Augustine's *Confessions: "Is not the life of man upon earth all trial?* Who wishes for troubles and difficulties? Thou commandest them to be endured, not to be loved." "In Thy Gift we rest; there we enjoy Thee. Our rest is our place . . . When out of order, they are restless; restored to order, they are at rest." "They be affections, they be loves; the uncleanness of our spirit flowing away downwards with the love of cares, and the holiness of Thine raising us upward by love of unanxious repose" (ed. Everyman's Libr., tr. E. B. Pusey [London, 1926], pp. 228, 313-315). The fundamental Augustinian concepts of desire and the point of repose recur as motifs in a number of variations throughout the *Persiles*. For example, both appear in Arnaldo's words of joy on discovering his beloved Auristela in Golandia: "Seas bien hallada, norte por donde se guían mis honestos pensamientos, y estrella fija que me lleva al puerto donde han de tener reposo mis buenos deseos" (p. 122). Similarly Auristela sees herself to be "el clavo de la rueda de su [Periandro] fortuna y la esfera del movimiento de sus deseos" (p. 473). Referring to her beloved, the tormented Isabela Castrucho asks: "¿No soy yo por ventura el centro donde reposan sus pensamientos? ¿No soy yo el blanco donde asestan sus deseos?" (p.

Although the *Persiles*, symbolically interpreted, can be seen as Cervantes' divine comedy, its actions are confined to the real world. It must be remembered that the work was conceived in terms of neoclassical literary theories, stressing the imitation of nature and maintaining that verisimilitude is one of the most important qualities in fiction.[27] There is here no entry into the Heavenly City nor a direct vision of God rewarding the pilgrims. The work ends rather with the restoration of peace and fertility to the northern kingdoms and the diffusion of Catholic enlightenment to their inhabitants. Moreover, the diabolical

---

410). A humorous interlude with the Spanish man of letters collecting aphorisms is the occasion for the restatement of the motif: "*No desees y serás el más rico hombre del mundo*" (p. 418). The sober narrator punctuates a downward turn in the fortunes of the protagonists: "Es tan poca la seguridad con que se gozan los humanos gozos, que nadie se puede prometer en ellos un mínimo punto de firmeza" (p. 473). Counseling Sinforosa in her love problems, Auristela remarks: ". . . bien sé que nuestras almas están siempre en continuo movimiento, sin que puedan dejar de estar atentas a querer bien a algún sujeto" (p. 170). It goes without saying that such fundamental principles underlying the creation of the *Persiles* were widely expressed in the literature of the Counter Reformation. Tasso describes the end of history and the repose of eternity (*Mondo creato*, VII, 418-426):

> E giusto è ben che s'allor fine avranno
> I moti de le stelle erranti e fisse,
> L'abbiano quelli ancor di mente e d'alma
> Umana, ch'assembrar del cielo il corso.
> Tutti avran pace allor nel fisso punto
> De la Divinità. Riposo eterno
> Sarà l'intender nostro e 'l nostro amore,
> Che in tante guise ora si varia e cangia,
> E con tante volubili rivolte.

[27] See my *Cervantes, Aristotle and the "Persiles,"* Chs. I, VIII.

forces and monsters, the "dragons" of the medieval fantasy, which the heroes must overcome, are only those whose existence the Renaissance mind accepted as possible in the natural order. Nevertheless, through traditional symbols and allusions to Christian and classical mythology, a mythic movement running parallel to the movement of the plot is established. Although the degree to which this movement approaches the surface of this high mimetic work varies, it is continuously present and sustains the total symbolic meaning of the events of the narration.[28]

For example, the goal of the pilgrims is Rome, which had been traditionally regarded not only as the center of the world but also as the simulacrum of the City of God (at one point in the *Persiles* Cervantes writes: "Roma es el cielo de la tierra" [p. 192]). The author reinforces the traditional association as the pilgrims ritualistically ascend a hill overlooking Rome, where they kneel in adoration of the goal of their quest "como a cosa sacra."[29] As Frye

[28] I use "high mimetic" here as Northrop Frye defines the term in his theory of modes (see *Anatomy of Criticism* [Princeton, 1957], pp. 33-34). More will be said of the "varying degree of presence" of the mythic below, and examples will be given.

[29] This scene reminds Farinelli ("El último sueño romántico de Cervantes," p. 134) of the scene in Tasso's *Gerusalemme liberata* in which the Christians contemplate the walls of Jerusalem (Canto III). The comparison is in my opinion very relevant; for the city, as the organizing principle for the action of the work, as a symbol of the heavenly kingdom, as a point of order in a world of suffering and deception, and, as goal of a quest and the emblematic representation of the moral values associated with that quest—faith in God, perseverance, and duty—has the same function in each work (see A. Bartlett Giamatti, *The Earthly Paradise and the Renaissance Epic* [Princeton, 1966], pp. 179-210).

points out, the hill is one of the archetypal locations for the point of epiphany, at which the "undisplaced apocalyptic world and the cyclical world of nature come into alignment."[30] Like the Bible, the *Persiles* presents several mountain-top epiphanies, and it is logical that in this, the most important of them, Cervantes would attempt to re-actualize the climactic moment of the Revelation when John the Divine is carried to a high mountain to observe the New Jerusalem descending from heaven. The archetypal hill and the traditional associations clustering around the city of Rome are not the only means by which Cervantes keeps the level of myth present in this scene. As they contemplate the Eternal City, the pilgrims overhear a poem which renders its relationship to the City of God, which has been introduced earlier into the context of the *Persiles* in Feliciana de la Voz's song describing the celestial paradise, explicit:

> No hay parte en ti [Rome] que no sirva de ejemplo
> de santidad, así como trazada
> de la ciudad de Dios al gran modelo.   (p. 426)

As we shall see, most of the poems in the *Persiles* establish a mythic background for the events of the narration and prescribe the direction in which an allegorical commentary on the fictions must proceed.

In what Renaissance literary theorists would regard as the major plot of the work, the *Persiles* consists of a sequence of adventures in which the young heroes must struggle with numerous antagonists, which are usually linked to demonic agencies. These adventures follow a cyclical pattern, as a moment of struggle, bondage, or

[30] *Anatomy of Criticism*, p. 203.

"near-death" alternates with a moment of resurrection or triumphant vision of the final goal of the quest. Thus all adventures repeat in miniature the circular pattern of the entire quest, which encompasses them. Quite appropriately in view of both the overall movement from the lower order of fallen man to the restored paradise which the *Persiles* symbolically represents and the *in-medias-res* structural technique perfected by Heliodorus and recommended by the theorists, Cervantes chooses to begin the *Persiles* at the lowest moment in the fortunes of the hero and the moment when he is most distant from the climactic vision of his goal from the hill and his return to his kingdom. Separated from his beloved Auristela, Periandro lies imprisoned in the depths of a cave on the island of the barbarians, where his heart is to be ripped out and devoured by his captors. In composing this scene, Cervantes was probably recalling the descriptions of such startling practices in sixteenth-century chronicles about the new world and its inhabitants. Moreover, he may have been following contemporary literary theories concerning the legitimate marvelous and specifically Tasso's suggestion that the poet describe the realities of the new world, which, although strange and wonderful, are verified by the historians and accepted as true by the reading public.[31] How-

[31] As Aristotle had observed that epic and tragedy should be both marvelous and verisimilar, Renaissance literary theorists devoted much attention to techniques and types of subject matter by which the poet could arouse *admiratio* without destroying the reader's faith in the possibility of the actions of the plot. They distinguished a legitimate marvelous from an illegitimate marvelous. The former is based on poetic language, structural elements such as peripeteia, variety in descriptions and subject matter, great historical occurrences, and the Christian supernatural. The latter arises from un-

ever, the marvelous detail has an important function within the symbolic rhythm of the *Persiles* and is the first of the various details showing how Cervantes assimilated contemporary history to his underlying theme. Cannibalism is an archetypal demonic motif in literature, and appearing here, it imaginatively links the hero's persecutors not only with the American Indians but also with the powers of hell.[32] The connections between barbarian society and Christian mythology are rendered more concrete in their prophecy, which associates them specifically with the false prophet and Antichrist of the Apocalypse. They are "persuadidos, o ya del demonio, o ya de un antiguo hechicero a quien ellos tienen por sapientísimo

---

controlled multiplicity in subject matter and violations of the laws of empirical reality which have no causes in the Christian supernatural. (See Forcione, *Cervantes, Aristotle, and the "Persiles,"* Ch. I.) Throughout the *Persiles* Cervantes employs only the legitimate marvelous. For Tasso's remarks about the new world, see *Del poema eroico*, p. 109.

[32] "It is consistent with this that the Eucharist symbolism of the apocalyptic world, the metaphorical identification of vegetable, animal, human, and divine bodies, should have the imagery of cannibalism for its demonic parody. Dante's last vision of human hell is of Ugolino gnawing his tormentor's skull" (Frye, *Anatomy of Criticism*, p. 148). Within the total context of the *Persiles* the barbarians' cannibalism represents the demonic perversion of the Holy Sacrament, which is introduced concretely and celebrated in one of the heroes' adventures in Spain (see below). Similarly the barbarians' grotesque marriage (the bridegroom must pass the test of swallowing a human heart without wincing) and its prophesied offspring, the conqueror of much of the world, are demonic counterweights of the various Christian marriages which the work celebrates and of the true Messiah.

varón, que de entre ellos ha de salir un rey que conquiste y gane gran parte del mundo" (p. 57). Subsequent references to the few good barbarians as angels reinforce the link between their demonic society and that of the fallen angels. The cave in which Periandro is imprisoned is described as "antes sepultura que prisión de muchos cuerpos vivos que en ella estaban sepultados." The isolation of the hero is revealed dramatically in his inability to understand the language of his captors, which is likened to "terrible estruendo." After Periandro's executioners have hoisted him from the dungeon and wiped the dust from his face, the beautiful youth "alzó el rostro, y miró al cielo, por todas partes" and thanks God for delivering him from the darkness of the cave and allowing him to see His light before his death. As if by providential design a storm suddenly delivers the youth from his captors, as the raging sea destroys their raft, drowns them, and bears Periandro to his rescue by the ship of Prince Arnaldo, in which he "volvió en sí, como de muerte a vida" (p. 54).

In the first scene of the romance we observe what we might call, using the terminology of the fugue, a complete statement of the subject and the answer of the major theme, which will be repeated endlessly with variations throughout the work. The motifs of bondage and deliverance, death and rebirth, darkness and light are sounded rapidly. The linkage of these archetypal motifs to a Christian context is obvious in Periandro's prayer; and hence we associate the darkness within which the hero lies with the realm of the demonic and the light of the heavens with the divine. Moreover, the numerous biblical allusions and motifs that appear in the narration of the following scenes allow us to see in the natural cataclysm which destroys the evil forces and delivers the chosen the Red Sea and the great flood of the Scriptures.

The pattern which begins the romance continues as Periandro immediately returns to the island of the barbarians to search for Auristela. There he finds his beloved in a similar situation, standing before her executioner awaiting the death blow. Again the heroes are miraculously delivered, as Periandro's beauty arouses a sodomitic passion in Bradamiro, a quarrel erupts between him and the other barbarians, and a blazing fire ravages the island. Periandro and Auristela wander lost amid the confusion around them. Again the motif of darkness appears at the moment of catastrophe: "... cerraba la noche, y como se ha dicho, escura y temerosa" (p. 69). But "heaven does not forget to come to their aid," and a young barbarian leads them along a tortuous path through a dark cavern to an illuminated refuge. As a second deliverer appears, Cervantes' description suggests very strongly that God's angels have guided the protagonists to safety, just as the angel and pillar of fire guided the elect through the wilderness before the pursuing armies of the Pharoah.

> —¡Bendito sea Dios—dijo el bárbaro en la misma lengua castellana—que nos ha traído a este lugar, que, aunque en él se puede temer algún peligro, no será de muerte!
>
> En esto vieron que hacia ellos *venía corriendo una gran luz, bien así como cometa* . . .
>
> —El cielo te pague, *ángel humano*, o quienquiera que seas . . .
>
> *Llegó en esto la luz*, que la traía uno al parecer bárbaro. . . (p. 70)

The young barbarian explains that an impulse sent from heaven prompted him to save the Christians from the fire and sword of their enemies, and the heroes observe in their escape one of God's miracles.

As in the first deliverance, we observe in the background a cosmic disaster of apocalyptic overtones, as the all-consuming flames (Sodom and Gomorrah, Jericho, the Apocalypse) devour the society of the barbarians and leave the chosen few, safely sheltered in their refuge, to endure a night which is longer than usual, as the smoke from the smouldering embers remains impenetrable to the rays of the rising sun,[33] and to continue in their quest. In the midst of the motifs of "near-death," imprisonment, darkness, fear, and natural disaster, the motif of physical death is sounded, but its tone points toward Christian resurrection and the goal of the "trabajos." The aged servant of Auristela dies, her "ojos clavados en el cielo, y casi quebrados," declaring: "yo muero cristiana en la fe de Jesucristo, y en la que tiene, que es la misma, la santa Iglesia católica romana" (p. 78).

From this moment of epiphany on, the motif of regeneration begins to dominate.[34] Up to this point the few

---

[33] "Tardó aquel día en mostrarse al mundo, al parecer, más de lo acostumbrado, a causa que el humo y pavesas del incendio de la isla, que aun duraba, impedía que los rayos del sol por aquella parte no pasasen a la tierra" (p. 79). Compare: ". . . he opened the shaft of the bottomless pit, and from the shaft rose smoke like the smoke of a great furnace, and the sun and the air were darkened with the smoke from the shaft" (Rev. 9:2).

[34] Cervantes' insertion of Cloelia's death at this point is startling, as nothing in the narration has pointed toward it and the author makes no effort to present a plausible cause of death. The incident, which has an emblematic quality, has a double function in the

details concerning the landscape of the island (rocks, crags, caves) have suggested ruggedness and sterility, reflecting the condition of its inhabitants and symbolically linking the island to the forces of evil. On emerging from the refuge on the morning following Cloelia's death, Periandro and Auristela behold in astonishment the fruit-bearing trees of a verdant circular area nourished by several fresh-water streams: ". . . estaba crecida la hierba, porque las muchas aguas que de las peñas salían las tenían en perpetua verdura" (p. 79). The geometrical configuration of hell—the labyrinth—has been replaced by the perfect form—the emblem of eternity; the salt waters of death, by the life-giving waters flowing down from the mountains; the demonic cave, by the earthly paradise.[35]

Antonio's wife resumes her history, describing her instruction in the Catholic faith by Antonio and her baptism in the waters of the mountain stream, and repeating the Credo. Her declaration of faith at this early moment in the romance offers a complete statement of the religious principles inspiring the *Persiles*: faith in God, the Son, and the Holy Spirit, obedience to the "santa Iglesia católica romana, regida por el Espíritu Santo y gobernada por el

---

symbolic movement of the work. Antonio, the deliverer of the heroes, is narrating his life story, and he has just described his escape from the sea, the moment of "near-death" and isolation in his expiatory quest (see below). This is hence the moment of his quest paralleling the present moment in the quest of Periandro and Auristela. Cloelia's death punctuates this parallelism of narrative threads and points toward the way of ascent in both quests. Her visionary experience is immediately repeated within Antonio's narration by the barbarian's wife Ricla. More will be said of the effects of such parallelism and repetition of motifs below.

[35] See Frye, *Anatomy of Criticism*, pp. 141-150.

Sumo Pontífice, vicario y visorrey de Dios en la tierra, sucesor legítimo de San Pedro, su primer pastor después de Jesucristo, primero y universal pastor de su esposa la Iglesia" (p. 82), faith in the Virgin, and the belief in the sanctity of Christian marriage and its fruits. The goal of the quest of the heroes is Christian instruction in the city of Rome and sacramental marriage following that instruction. Ricla's words here point toward the realization of their goals and foreshadow the words of instruction which Auristela will hear at the conclusion of their journey. Following Ricla's account the remaining captives in the dungeon-cavern, in which Periandro began his adventures among the barbarians, are delivered from its darkness; the small group kneels at the shore, prays to God for guidance, and sets out in the boats of their captors with high hopes of reaching civilization.

In addition to revealing rapidly and directly the Christian themes of the romance, the opening adventures of the *Persiles* demonstrate very clearly the cyclical process which is to recur throughout the work. The heroes must struggle against an adversary and overcome him in order to continue in their quest. In their struggle they must endure a momentary defeat (imprisonment, "near-death," passage through the labyrinth or the purgatorial fires) before their triumph, and their triumph is generally rewarded with a moment of vision of the goal of the quest. Thus Periandro's uplifted gaze and prayer, Cloelia's gaze toward heaven in death, and Ricla's recitation of the Credo are the first of a series of intermediary visionary moments which follow on the upward turn of the recurrent cycle and lead toward the climactic vision of Rome from the hill.

Angus Fletcher has observed that allegorical literature often moves through a series of such epiphanies toward a final one and has employed Eliade's term the "symbol of the center" to describe these moments. The term is, I think, particularly applicable to the *Persiles*, in which all characters are in search of a "punto" and discover that the only point which ultimately quiets the desire driving them forward in their quests is to be found at the true "centro" of the universe, God. ". . . we find that central to most such rituals [Fletcher is referring here to the ritualistic character of allegorical composition] there are special moments of particular exuberance, particular intensity, particular vision, and these moments involve what we have called 'symbols of the center.' To recall the main criterion: from the spatial point of view such a symbol, as Eliade has described it, would be a temple or indeed any sacred place to which the hero is drawn and in which he receives his initiation into the vision of his true destiny. . . . It appears that any temporal moment of particular intensity can serve as a symbol of the center, or, putting it another way, just as space is "sacred space" in the Temple, so time is "sacred time" in the Temple, while we can sometimes be shown a moment of sacred time without any of the spatial trappings that go to make up a proper temple. Interpreted somewhat freely, these notions allow a wide variety of things and experiences to possess the qualities of holiness."[36] Thus the shore from which Periandro gazes

[36] Angus Fletcher: *Allegory, The Theory of a Symbolic Mode* (Ithaca, N.Y., 1964), pp. 350-351, hereafter cited as "Fletcher." See also Otto F. Bollnow, *Mensch und Raum* (Stuttgart, 1963), pp. 141-143; Mircea Eliade, *Das Heilige und das Profane* (Hamburg, 1957), Chs. I-II.

toward heaven following his emergence from the underground dungeon and Antonio's hidden refuge and circular garden are spatial settings for the "temple experience," and they will be recreated often in the *Persiles*; the hermitage of Renato, the temples of Lisbon, the monastery of Guadalupe, the cave of Soldino, the church of Valencia, and the hill overlooking Rome are the most important. If Periandro's prayer begins the series of triumphant visions, his cave-dungeon introduces a series of negative symbols of the center, which mark the lowest point in the downward turn of the recurrent cycle.[37] Generally oppressive, enclosing space is the dominant characteristic of the many recreations of the place of bondage in the *Persiles*, e.g., the various prisons, the hollow hill, the ship-leviathan, the hollow tree trunk of Feliciana, the chamber of Hipólita, and the small boat of Antonio, but they can often be created in less conventional spatial circumstances, e.g., the islands of ice, the palace of Policarpo, and the dark alleys of Lisbon, which become a labyrinth for Ortel Banedre.

The *Persiles* moves endlessly back and forth between the positive and the negative symbol of the center, reenacting ritualistically the Christian eschatological vision of bondage and restoration in the same way in which it is reenacted symbolically in the Revelation, where the vision

---

[37] "Such a positive value cannot always be ascribed to the symbol of the center. Literature and, unfortunately, history have presented the opposite kind of sacred place, and we commonly call it 'hell.' Prisons are such places, in fact or in imaginative 'prison literature.'" In these places we discover "a terrible alienation from the comic world of love, marriage, dance, and merriment" (Fletcher, pp. 213-214).

of the city of Babylon yields to the triumphant vision of the New Jerusalem. Accompanying the respective moments of this cyclical movement between the upper and lower centers are the motifs of struggle-triumph, bondage-deliverance, darkness-light, sterility-fertility, death-resurrection, all of which are resonant with overtones of traditional Christianity. Thus there is usually a suggestion through allusion, imagery, and symbol that in the struggle of the heroes divine and demonic forces are in combat and that the heroes' quest is analogous to that of God's Elect in the Bible.

The continuous reenactment of the same ritual in the *Persiles* produces that effect of timelessness which normally attends ritualistic activity, that "abolition of time through the imitation of archetypes and the repetition of paradigmatic gestures," to which Eliade refers in his discussion of the ontological conception of primitive man.[38] This effect is in large part the result of the endless recurrence of the specific motifs which accompany the respective moments of the cycle. We have the feeling that each episode and each adventure, regardless of who is involved, whether the setting is the stark landscape of the north or the civilized world of southern Europe,[39] and whether the

[38] Mircea Eliade, *The Myth of the Eternal Return: or, Cosmos and History*, tr. W. Trask, Princeton/Bollingen Paperback no. 258 (Princeton, 1971), p. 35.

[39] In my opinion, Cervantists have placed for too much emphasis on the differences between the first and the second part of the *Persiles*. While the Christian mythology is generally less displaced in the northern adventures than in the southern adventures, the *morisco* episode, the occurrences in the temple of Guadalupe, and the arrival in Rome all demonstrate that it can approach the surface

46

subject matter assimilated to the underlying ritual is historical or literary—biblical, classical, or chivalric—contain all that has gone before and all that will come afterward.[40] Moreover, by rapid shifts from motifs surrounding one

---

of the action just as in the most "symbolic" of the northern scenes. At the same time we observe in most of the adventures in Policarpo's kingdom a displacement of myth which is essentially the same as that in many of the "realistic" southern scenes. The traditional distinction between a symbolical and a realistic half of the *Persiles*, which survives in Casalduero's observation of a distinction between the imagination and reality, myth and history, in the northern and southern adventures respectively, ignores the fact that the second half of the work continues to reactualize the Christian mythology and employs the symbolic methods of the first half to do so (see *Sentido y forma de "Los trabajos de Persiles y Sigismvnda"* [Buenos Aires, 1947], pp. 173 ff.). Walter Boehlich is correct when he points to certain similarities between the northern and southern adventures and suggests that the traditional distinction between them is invalid ("Heliodorus Christianus: Cervantes und der byzantinische Roman," *Freundesgabe für Ernst Robert Curtius* [Bern, 1956], pp. 103-124).

[40] "Das Leitmotiv lässt in Musik und Dichtkunst Früheres wiederanklingen, um Zusammenhänge gefühlsmässig zu versinnlichen. Es gibt ein inhaltliches Mehr" (Oskar Walzel, *Wechselseitige Erhellung der Künste* [Berlin, 1917], p. 78). The effect of Cervantes' motifs in the *Persiles* is analogous to that which Bach would achieve in music and that for which Wagner would strive and on which he would base his theory of the *Leitmotiv* two centuries later. "Es war *Wagners* Griff, dass er mitt Bewusstsein auch die *Einheit der Zeitlichen Trennung* in der Musik hören lassen wollte, das Ineinander auch des vergangenen und kommenden Lebens in der konkreten Gegenwart. In dem Durchtönen der Motive . . . ist die Lebenstiefe des konkreten Zusammenhanges unseres Daseins in jedem erfüllten Augenblick gegenwärtig, diese mystische Zeiteinheit unserer Existenz, wo jede Gegenwart 'schwanger ist mit der Zukunft' und alle Vergangenheit in ihr 'aufgehoben,' im

moment of the cycle to those surrounding the other, and, what is more important, by the occasional intermingling of motifs from the respective moments, Cervantes succeeds in producing an effect not of *succession* but rather of *simultaneity* of moments within the cyclical movement of the ritual itself. For example, amid the dominant motifs of death, isolation, and darkness, the single motif of distant stars will sound to maintain the other moment of the cycle as present; during the festivity celebrating the restoration of separated lovers and marriage, the motif of death will emerge in a dark undertone. Such polyphony[41] is thematically important; for it underscores the interdependence of both moments of the cycle and the preservation of the moment of bondage and evil in the moment

---

tiefsten Sinne alles zugleich. In der grossartigsten Weise hat schon *Bach* so mit dem Mittel der Musik gearbeitet" (Herman Nohl, *Die Ästhetische Wirklichkeit* [Frankfurt am Main, 1954], pp. 175-176).

[41] Here too music offers an effective analogy for describing this type of effect. Nohl writes that of the various artistic media music best achieves the "Vereinheitlichung der Mehrheit des Ausdrucks in der einen Harmonie. Das ist der innerste Sinn der Polyphonie. Am stärksten fühlen wir dieses Ineinander des Auseinander. . . ." He writes of Bach's music: "Das Entscheidende dabei ist doch . . . dass die Gegensätze, hier von gesetzhafter und evangelischer Anschauung vom Tode, nicht als dramatischer Konflikt zweier Mächte erscheinen, wo dann die eine überwunden würde, sondern sie stehen bis zuletzt nebeneinander, *das geschichtliche Nacheinander ist zuinnerst ein Ineinander*, das religiöse Wesen ist die Spannung von einem zum andern und zugleich ihre Aufhebung, hegelsch geredet, 'die Rose im Kreuz der Gegenwart' " (*Die Ästhetische Wirklichkeit*, pp. 173-177; see also *Stil und Weltanschauung* [Jena, 1920], p. 113).

of liberation, i.e., the value of "los trabajos." In the words of the sage, Mauricio: ". . . las buenas andanzas no vienen sin el contrapeso de desdichas, las cuales tienen jurisdición y un modo de licencia de entrarse por los buenos sucesos, para darnos a entender que, ni el bien es eterno, ni el mal durable" (p. 116). The discursive narrator returns to this theme, employing the image which recurs so often in the work, the spatial point at which all converges: "Parece que el bien y el mal distan tan poco el uno del otro, que son como dos líneas concurrentes, que aunque parten de apartados y diferentes principios, acaban en un punto" (p. 464). We observe here, in addition to a metaphorical statement of the necessity of evil in God's providential order, an effective geometrical analogy of the union of opposites in a higher synthesis which underlies the Christian vision of fall and redemption and the ritual which reactualizes this vision repeatedly in the *Persiles*.[42]

It is curious that Cervantes shows a great deal of concern with chronological time in the *Persiles*, often informing his reader of the number of days which pass as his heroes wander from location to location. Such comments are one of various elements which reveal the importance of the author's neoclassical literary theories in the composition of the work, for the references to time of travel, just like the references to real geography, are made in the interest of verisimilitude. (A modern commentator has observed that, in view of the location of the "mar helado" and the Categat, Cervantes' statements that Periandro's journey

---

[42] See also ". . . las dichas y las desdichas suelen andar tan juntas, que tal vez no hay medio que las divida; andan el pesar y el placer tan apareados . . ." (p. 162).

between these points lasted a month and covered four hundred leagues are those of a skilled geographer.) [43] Despite Cervantes' concern for temporal plausibility, the references to chronological time in the *Persiles* seem to be inappropriate and nonfunctional; that is to say, the work remains fundamentally atemporal and ahistorical. [44] It is the visionary moment rather than the duration of his-

[43] Ricardo Beltrán y Rózpide, "La pericia geográfica de Cervantes demonstrada con la 'Historia de los Trabajos de Persiles y Sigismunda,'" *Boletín de la Real Sociedad Geográfica*, 64 (1923), 286-287.

[44] The peculiar coexistence of geographical exactness and symbolic space in the *Persiles* is analogous. As will be pointed out below, the symbolic nature of the various settings described thoroughly eclipses their reality as measurable or geographical space. Several studies have shown that Cervantes reveals a thorough knowledge of contemporary geography in his work. Indeed all his locations can be found on maps of the age, even such seemingly fantastic places as the Island of Fire and the Island of the Hermits. However, in one notable case the importance of symbolic space causes Cervantes to sacrifice absolute geographical precision and verisimilitude. Rome, as "cabeza del mundo," "Eternal City," and a real city, was well-suited to be the goal of Cervantes' heroes. However, those maps of the time that had the greatest pretensions to scientific accuracy offered no city or country with such symbolic power for the origins of the quest. Hence Cervantes turns to classical geography, locating Periandro's kingdom on Thule. He underscores its traditional associations as a hallowed kingdom and "the end of the earth" by introducing Virgil's ". . . Ac tua nautae/ Numina sola colant: tibi serviat ultima Thule" (p. 465). At the same time the author is careful to legitimize the momentary lapse, as shortly after the allusion, a character says: ". . . Tule, que agora vulgarmente se llama Islanda. . ." (p. 469). (See my remarks below on the occasional tension between the verisimilar and the symbolic in the *Persiles*.)

tory, the exemplary and essential in man rather than the individual (i.e., "character"), the paradigmatic gesture rather than unique or new human activity, and the symbolic rather than the individuating gaze on the external world which form the fabric of Cervantes' final work. It was in the *Quixote* that Cervantes conceived of the ingenious idea of juxtaposing the archetypal, timeless reality characteristic of the world of literary romance to historical reality. In doing so he founded a new genre of literature, a genre based on all that the *Persiles* rejected—in a word, history.[45] To seek the novelistic in the *Persiles* is just as idle as to censure it for its failure to be novelistic.

TWO POTENTIAL OBJECTIONS

As I am proposing an allegorical reading of the *Persiles,* I would like to deal at this point with two potential objections to my critical approach. The first is Cervantes' apparent lack of theoretical interest in allegory and his failure to state that his work is allegorical. In fact, nearly all of Cervantes' allusions to allegory and methods of allegorical interpretation are sharply satirical. In the unforgettable young scholar who accompanies Don Quixote

[45] "Cervantes desplazó el acento, que hasta entonces apuntaba hacia la 'esencia' de la figura literaria, y lo puso sobre el tenso y problemático proceso vital de aquélla; sobre ésta se proyectan, con sus luces cambiantes, las acciones suyas y las de quienes forman con ella una textura humana de vida enlazada y entrechocada" (Américo Castro, *Cervantes y los casticismos españoles* [Barcelona, 1966], p. 21). See also Raymond S. Willis' excellent observations on Cervantes' revolutionary treatment of the dimension of time in the *Quixote* (*The Phantom Chapters of the Quijote* [New York, 1953], pp. 14-15). Considered in the context of literary history, the *Persiles* is certainly a much more *conservative* work than the *Quixote*.

to the cave of Montesinos (II, xxii-xxiv), Cervantes criticizes the tendency of the humanist culture to make knowledge an end in itself and to rely enthusiastically and slavishly on books as the sole source of wisdom. At the same time Cervantes employs the pedant in order to address himself to certain literary problems. Obsessed by the desire to confront books as repositories of facts, the youth forgets that there is a boundary separating the realm of the imagination from empirical reality.[46] His literary activity is the logical result of his obsession. He is a master of allegorical composition and is writing the *Ovidio español,* which will reveal, among other things, who the Giralda of Seville and the fountains of Lavapiés, el Piojo, and la Priora were in reality. Similar thrusts at the intricacies of contemporary allegorical readings are to be found in Diego de Miranda's scornful reference to the scholars who spend days in attempting to discover "si se han de entender de una manera o otra tales y tales versos de Virgilio" (II, 648-649) and in Don Quixote's criticism of his author and assertion: ". . . así debe de ser mi historia, que tendrá necesidad de comento para entenderla" (II, 562). Cervantes' most important burlesque of allegory, however, occurs in the *Coloquio de los perros.* Cipión introduces the question of allegorical interpretation in discussing the prophetic poem of the witch la Camacha. After defining the "sentido alegórico" ("el cual sentido no quiere decir lo que la letra suena, sino otra cosa que, aunque diferente, le haga

---

[46] In *Cervantes, Aristotle, and the "Persiles,"* I suggest that the cousin's failure to recognize this boundary is the same error as that made frequently by sixteenth-century literary theorists in their empirical interpretation of Aristotle's concept of verisimilitude (see Ch. IV).

semejanza"),[47] he proceeds to offer an interpretation of the stanza that is utterly ridiculous.

On the one hand Cervantes' ridicule of allegory can be seen as an example of his tendency to place all literary theorizing in a humorous context.[48] On the other hand his skeptical attitude is typical of the entire neo-Aristotelian literary school.[49] As El Pinciano's Ugo says: "No tengo

---

[47] See *Obras completas*, p. 1019. The definition recalls Carvallo's discussion of allegory. After distinguishing the *sound* of the words of a poem, which appeal to the faculty of the imagination, from the significance of the words, which is grasped by the faculty of the intellect, the theorist claims that poets occasionally use fictions as opposed to historical realities (e.g., the Bible) in their allegories: "Otras cosas ay que verdaderamente no fueron, sino que por alguna semejança se traen para significar alguna cosa. . . ." (*Cisne de Apolo*, ed. A. Porqueras Mayo [Madrid, 1958], I, 102).

[48] See *Cervantes, Aristotle, and the "Persiles,"* passim. Such expressions of skepticism about allegorical exegesis were common in the age. Montaigne wonders whether Homer "intended to say all that he has been made to say" and Ben Jonson refers to "those common Torturers, that bring all wit to the Rack: whose Noses are ever like Swine spoyling, and rooting up the *Muses* Gardens" (see Rhodes Dunlap, "The Allegorical Interpretation of Renaissance Literature," *PMLA*, 82 [1967], 39-43).

[49] That Cervantes employs personified abstractions in the pageants of Camacho's wedding, the fisherman's wedding, and Periandro's dream, and that in the prologue to this theatrical work he boasts of being "el primero que representase las imaginaciones y los pensamientos escondidos del alma, sacando figuras morales a teatro" (*Obras completas*, p. 180) do not contradict his disapproval of allegory as revealed in the contexts cited above. Such personifications do not represent the type of allegory which preoccupied Renaissance literary theorists. They were concerned with allegory primarily as a figure which conceals or obscures meaning and demands difficult "decoding." The literal meaning of the term as "other speech" was very much present in their interpretation;

doctrina de Aristóteles en esta materia poética [allegory],"[50] and little theoretical energy was wasted upon it by Renaissance interpreters of the *Poetics*. By and large they considered "allegorical meaning" to be fragmentary pieces of natural and moral philosophy concealed behind the fictions of a literary plot rather than an organized thought system which generates and is embedded in the very structure of the work. For them allegory is an accessory rather than an intrinsic part of the work. Moreover, as allegorical exegesis had been used traditionally as a way of justifying literature of questionable moral tone and plausibility, the Aristotelians tended to view allegory as incompatible with the highest quality in a literary work —namely, verisimilitude.[51]

---

for example, G. B. Pigna claimed that the "allegorical lie" exists to "bury" ("seppellire") truth (see *I romanzi* [Venice, 1554], p. 22) and Carvallo asserted that the aim of allegory is to make interpretation of exalted doctrine difficult (see op. cit., I, 113 ff.). It is interesting that El Pinciano discusses personifications of the type which Cervantes employs and does not refer to them as allegory (see op. cit., III, 294-296). Carvallo calls such personifications of abstractions "fabulas Metaphisicas" (I, 82), but does not mention them in his lengthy discussion of allegory. It should be pointed out, however, that on one occasion Cervantes does allude seriously and favorably to the allegorical methods as defined by the theorists. In attempting to dissuade Anselmo from his foolish test of his wife's fidelity, Lotario recalls Ariosto's story of the magic cup (*Furioso*, XLIII; this is the literary source of Cervantes' tale) and says: ". . . puesto que aquello sea ficción poética, tiene en sí encerrados secretos morales dignos de ser advertidos y entendidos e imitados" (*Don Quijote de la Mancha*, I, 334-335).

[50] Op. cit., III, 174.

[51] See Robert L. Montgomery, Jr., "Allegory and the Incredible Fable," *PMLA*, 81 (1966), 45-55.

El Pinciano's reasoning on the matter is typical of the entire school. He sees allegory as an independent type of literature only in one of the "minor species" of poetry— the "apólogo," or moral fable. In the "major species" it is something external, added on by the poet ("está como acessoria," "este apólogo o alegoría está sembrado en gran parte de las principales especies de la poética, principalmente en la épica").[52] El Pinciano claims that the great epic poems must utilize allegory and do so without sacrificing verisimilitude. Here he clearly refers to fragmentary pieces of moral and natural philosophy of the type which for centuries scholars had unearthed in the ancient epics and which Renaissance commentators discovered in Ariosto's *Orlando Furioso*.[53] However, his association of allegory with the nonverisimilar and hence with inferior art is evident on several occasions. He writes: ". . . el poeta que guarda la imitación y verisimilitud, guarda más la perfeción poética; y el que, dexando ésta, va tras la alegoría, guarda más la philosóphica doctrina; y assí digo de Homero y de los demás, que, si alguna vez por la alegoría dexaron la imitación, lo hizieron como philósophos y no como poetas, como lo hizo Esopo con otros que han escrito apólogos, cuyas narraciones son disparates y fríuolas. . . ."[54]

[52] Op. cit., III, 247.

[53] See III, 175-176. El Pinciano's phrase "sacar alegorías" (III, 167), describing the process of allegorical interpretation, just like his phrase "sembrar alegorías," describing the process of allegorical composition, suggests the unessential nature of allegory in this theory.

[54] Ibid., II, 95. See also his references to allegory as "burlas" and "disparates" as well as his conclusion of a discussion of allegory with the assertion that verisimilitude is the most important quality in literature (III, 249-250).

Like El Pinciano, Tasso devotes very little theoretical attention to allegory. Although at various stages in his career he resorts to allegorical readings to justify implausibilities and offenses against strict morality in his poetry, in his poetic theory he presents allegory as one of the rhetorical figures, very similar to enigma in its effect of mystery, asserts that it is an accidental rather than an essential quality of poetry, and shows little sympathy for a poet's sacrificing verisimilitude in his use of the figure.[55]

That Cervantes would have almost certainly denied that the *Persiles* is an allegory simply means that he considered verisimilitude to be the most important quality of a work of literature and that he viewed allegory as a distinct kind of literature and irreconcilable with verisimilar fiction. His view is that of his epoch. Montgomery writes: "By the end of the period it is difficult, if not impossible, to find a critic who does not consider allegory a special kind of literature rather than a quality inherent in all imaginative works which attempt to be meaningful . . . there is an established recognition that historical, believable materials are not the medium of allegory, that allegory is almost invariably associated with the false, the impossible, the incredible. . . ."[56] Cervantes' unfavorable references to allegory should then be understood in the context of contemporary literary theorizing, with its limited comprehension of the symbolical workings of literature, and should not be taken as a caveat against an illumination of the *Persiles* through analysis in terms of modern concepts of allegorical art. As the preceding section makes clear, when I speak of allegorical meaning, movement,

[55] See *Del poema eroico*, pp. 210-213.
[56] Montgomery, pp. 46, 55.

and structure in the *Persiles*, I am referring to something far different from what Renaissance theorists mean when they speak of allegory.

The second objection presents greater difficulties. Certainly one of the most important dimensions of the *Persiles* is the interest and suspense which are aroused by the adventures which compose its plot. It should be recalled that Cervantes referred to his masterpiece as a "libro de entretenimiento" and planned it as a modern version of the romance of chivalry, an essentially nonthematic form of fiction. It was with this in mind that W. Entwistle criticized the elaborate allegorical interpretation of the work by Casalduero.[57] To a certain extent I share Entwistle's objections. Casalduero's study, which presents brilliant insights into the symbolic workings of the *Persiles*, suffers in its attempt to impose a Procrustean scheme, vaguely designated as "the baroque," on the work. It forces many details into this pattern, neglects others entirely which cannot be cut to the required measurements (e.g., the importance of erudite commentary and ornamental descriptions and the function of literary theory in the work), and fails to acknowledge the importance of the pure entertainment

[57] Review of Casalduero's *Sentido y forma de "Los trabajos de Persiles y Sigismvnda," Modern Language Review*, 43 (1948), 426-429. Entwistle's critical judgment does no justice to the symbolic dimension of Cervantes' work. Moreover, implicit in his reading are traditional literary values which are, in my opinion, not relevant to an objective evaluation of the *Persiles*: on the one hand, a neo-Aristotelian notion of literary unity, on the other, the touchstone of most criticism of the prose narrative: character. Consequently he finds the *Persiles* episodic and its protagonists boring people, whose reality is given directly by the author and does not emerge from their actions within a real world.

residing in an adventure story, an aspect of the *Persiles* summarized and peremptorily dismissed as "Byzantinism." The problem is to what extent we are justified in going beyond the surface of adventure to an allegorical meaning. Fletcher writes that the "whole point of allegory is that it does not *need* to be read exigetically; it often has a literal level that makes good enough sense all by itself."[58] The problem is particularly acute in the genre which the *Persiles* represents: "This difficulty reaches an extreme in the study of romance forms, since most romances are read primarily for the adventure, and the fast-moving story is often sufficiently glittering to keep attention away from any underlying allegorical message."[59]

I think the difficulty can be overcome and the extremes marked by Entwistle's and Casalduero's interpretations avoided by recognizing at the outset that the allegorical density of romance is frequently not uniform and by utilizing the insights of two recent analysts of the workings of allegorical literature. Since the allegorical meaning of the *Persiles*—the movement of universal history and the destiny of the individual soul as understood by the Christian religion—is sustained by the conventional associations of specific biblical and classical myths which Cervantes in-

[58] Fletcher, p. 7. Fletcher is referring principally to the type of allegory which Frye ("Allegory," *Princeton Encyclopedia of Poetry and Poetics*, ed. Alex Preminger [Princeton, 1965], p. 12) designates as "complex," in which the author's interest in the "other," simultaneous structure of events or ideas which are referred to continuously by a fictional plot does not prevent his giving the plot an independent existence and value. In "simple" allegory, on the other hand, the plot is entirely subordinate to and occasionally obscured by the "other meaning."

[59] Fletcher, p. 313.

troduces at various points in his narration of the protagonists' adventures, Northrop Frye's concept of "displacement" is particularly helpful, for it allows us to speak of degrees to which the mythical background of a work may be present at different individual moments of the work. "Myth, then, is one extreme of literary design; naturalism is the other, and in between lies the whole area of romance, using that term romance to mean . . . the tendency . . . to displace myth in a human direction and yet, in contrast to 'realism,' to conventionalize content in an idealized direction. The central principle of displacement is that what can be metaphorically identified in a myth can only be linked in romance by some form of simile: analogy, significant association, incidental accompanying imagery, and the like."[60] At the same time Angus Fletcher writes of "loosening the boundaries of the mode," illustrating that in allegorical works there are often movements running counter to the allegorical movement, e.g., the mimetic and the ornamental, which may at individual moments override the allegorical understructure.[61]

Such notions allow us to deal with variations in the allegorical texture of the *Persiles* which might otherwise strike us as troublesome inconsistencies and tempt us to overinterpret.[62] In some cases the mythic movement is

[60] Frye, *Anatomy of Criticism*, pp. 136-137.

[61] Fletcher, pp. 312-315.

[62] Quite apart from his failure to recognize the unevenness in the allegorical texture of a romance such as the *Persiles*, the weakness in Casalduero's exegesis itself lies in his hypostatization of a "baroque reader," whose mind actively seeks Christian paradigms and analogies for all phenomena which it experiences. The unlimited store of associations alive in such a mind then supplies the critic with a vast context for his exegesis of the *Persiles*. The re-

clearly visible but accompanies other equally important thematic tendencies[63] (e.g., the erudite-informative or the satirical) and artistic processes (e.g., ornamental description or comedy of situation). For example, in the episodes

---

sult is, on the one hand, a confusing multiplication of meanings (e.g., the group of pilgrims huddling in Antonio's refuge as the island of the barbarians burns is both the primitive Christian Church and the church of the Counterreformation, menaced respectively by the fires of paganism and Protestantism; the differences between the maidens Sinforosa and Auristela are analogous to those between Catholicism and Protestantism), on the other hand, a fragmentation of the *Persiles* into discrete units, each the point of departure for a rambling excursus. It seems to me that, if it is to be successful, allegorical exegesis must take as its point of departure only what is *within* the work. Such a method reveals a *Persiles* which is thematically much simpler and structurally much more skillfully designed than that which Casalduero's work describes.

[63] I should emphasize that what I am discussing in this study by no means exhausts the thematic substance of the *Persiles*. I am dealing with the underlying organization of the work (the quest, the ritualistic cycle) and the way in which the spirit of orthodox Christianity animates this structure. The work is encyclopedic, containing information on a wide variety of topics (cosmology, physiology, geography, demonology, astrology, lycanthropy, courtly conduct, love, jealousy, statecraft, etc.), in addition to occasional satire, and hence it can be read in a variety of ways. For example, Alberto Sánchez has read it as a Renaissance manual for moral conduct, extracting its numerous *sententiae* and organizing them under such fundamental categories as "Amor y Celos" and "Religión" ("El 'Persiles' como repertorio de moralidades," *Anales Cervantinos*, 4 [1954], 199-223). In *Cervantes, Aristotle, and the "Persiles,"* I have studied one of its most interesting thematic dimensions, that of literary theory and its own literary reality. On the encyclopedic aspect of the *Persiles*, see P. Savj-Loópez, *Cervantes*, tr. A. Solalinde (Madrid, 1917), p. 216.

of Periandro's dream and the counterfeit captives' recitation, the reenactment of the basic myth of the *Persiles*, in both cases in a fictional context, coexists with concerns of literary theory, comedy of situation, and ornamental description. In other cases the mythic movement recedes and is present only by implication. For example, Golandia is a place of deliverance, and as such could become one of the many positive symbols of the center of the work, a setting for the triumphant vision of the destination of the wanderers. The kingdom is described as a huge mountain offering a port to the desperate pilgrims, who, on arriving, make the surprising discovery that "era de católicos." However, Cervantes does not proceed to develop the symbolic possibilities of the setting and is more interested in using the occasion for a description of the harbor, the hospice, and the marvelous bird which the dwellers of the island raise,[64] a discussion of astrology, and moralizing discourses on the evils of the satiric poet and the power of lustful women to control monarchs. Similarly in the extended adventure with King Policarpo, court intrigues,

[64] The narrator's words introducing the description of how the dwellers of the northern lands implant stakes at the edge of the ocean, which in the process of decay engender the delicious bird called barnaclas, reveal clearly the presence of certain tendencies in the work which are not necessarily connected with its allegorical movement—the informative and the marvelous: ". . . satisficieron todos la hambre, más con muchos géneros de pescados que con carnes, porque no sirvió otra que la de muchos pájaros, que se crían en aquellas partes, de tan extraña manera, que por ser rara y peregrina, me obliga a que aquí la cuente" (p. 110). To be recalled are Tasso's recommendations that the poet employ the customs of the northern lands to embellish his poem with marvelous subject matter.

61

problems of love, and statecraft completely overshadow the symbolic role of the island kingdom as place-of-salvation–place-of-bondage. And finally in other cases the level of plausible, fast-moving adventure is so dominant that the mythic movement vanishes altogether. As I shall point out below, many of the adventures contained in Periandro's recitation fall into this category.

One of the most interesting phenomena in the *Persiles* is the tension that arises occasionally as the mimetic and the mythic come into open conflict. As if suddenly aware of the variations which we observe in the texture, the narrator appears to remind the reader that what is happening is plausible and in effect underscores the fact that there is displacement. In other words the "censor principle," which is always at work in displacement, and, one would think, would have to be concealed if the process were to be effective, is jarringly visible throughout the *Persiles*. It is the voice of the Canon of Toledo and the entire neo-Aristotelian critical movement, which in the name of imitation is ever ready to pull the author down to earth. In these cases Cervantes' major aesthetic preoccupation, verisimilitude, remains unshaken, and we witness a peculiar simultaneous introduction and negation of myth. Admittedly Cervantes' notions of the plausible were far broader than those of the novelists of the modern realist school. Nevertheless, his determination to avoid any violations of probability is essentially the same as theirs, and he is often concerned when the symbolic ingredients and the arbitrary causation of the ritual which his plot repeatedly enacts threaten to conflict manifestly with the principle of probability. His authorizations of plausibility range from numerous arbitrary statements of his narrator to the effect that what is happening is not miraculous[65] to extended digressions which reflect on the problematic plausibility of an element of the plot (e.g., the discussion of lycanthropy, among other things, legitimizes both the transformation of Rutilio's witch into a wolf and the marvelous talking wolf which Antonio has encountered earlier in the work), to the traditional device of the dream vision, which renders plausible the only direct entry of the undisplaced mythic order into the world of the *Persiles* and the only case in which Cervantes momentarily resorts to "simple" allegory, the masque contained in Periandro's narration.

[65] The narrator intervenes to assure us that a capsized ship can stay afloat: ". . . que le puede suceder a un bajel" (p. 161); that, when the pilgrims kindle a fire by rubbing sticks together, they are employing an "artificio tan sabido como usado" (p. 98); that two ships can take advantage of a steady wind to embark in opposite directions: ". . . iban las naves con un mismo viento, por diferentes caminos, que éste es uno de los que parecen misterios en el arte de la navegación" (p. 276); that a woman's survival of a fall from a tower is a ". . . cosa posible, sin ser milagro" (p. 373). See other examples below.

CHAPTER TWO

Plot

THE CHIAROSCUROS OF THE NORTHERN ADVENTURES

THE symbolic rhythm of the opening scenes of the *Persiles* is repeated in most of the adventures which compose the major plot of the work. Following their departure from the smoldering kingdom of the barbarians, the pilgrims row to a nearby island where they spend a sleepless night, menaced by the bitter cold and fearful for their survival. In the dim light of morning, they discover that they have put ashore at an uninhabited wasteland of ice, and, as the weather worsens, they return to the sea. Amid the familiar motifs of darkness, isolation, sterility, and fear, the visionary note sounds once again, recalling Cloelia's Christian death and Ricla's recital of the Credo as the barbarians' fires raged outside the cavern refuge. The Portuguese gentleman, Manuel de Sosa Coitiño, one of the prisoners released from the dungeon, sings a love sonnet, celebrating the virtues of love, hope, constancy, perseverance, and chastity, and employing the traditional image of the ship of life guided by such virtues through the dangers of the sea to a happy port:

> Mar sesgo, viento largo, estrella clara,
> camino, aunque no usado, alegre y cierto,
> al hermoso, al seguro, al capaz puerto
> llevan la nave vuestra, única y rara.   (p. 96)

The elements echo the spirit of the song: the sea becomes tranquil, allowing the movements of the oars to accompany the singer in an even cadence and propel the boat to an island covered with trees which offer fruit, wood for a fire, and branches for a hut. The pilgrims spend a comfortable night in the refuge ("pareciéndoles aquella choza dilatado alcázar") and witness in the narration of Manuel de Sosa Coitiño's unrequited love a vision of mystical love binding man and God. In its color, music, and pageantry the wedding of Coitiño's beloved and Christ is the most spectacular of the visionary moments of the northern adventures, and it looks forward to the final scenes of the work and the actual experiences of the protagonists in the temples of Spain and Italy. As it introduces the true Messiah and describes the true marriage—man and God— it forms a counterweight to the diabolical marriage of the barbarians and its offspring, who, like the Antichrist, is expected to bring the entire world under his dominion.[1]

After burying Sosa Coitiño in the ice and leaving a small cross to mark the site, the wanderers return to the sea, which they now find to be "sosegado y blando," and

---

[1] The introduction of the tale of Manuel de Sosa Coitiño is of biographical interest, as Cervantes probably knew the Portuguese poet during their captivity in Algiers (see Wolfgang Kayser, *Das Sprachliche Kunstwerk* [Bern, 1962], pp. 373-374). It is possible that Cervantes chose this figure in order to introduce, perhaps with humorous intent, a current literary topic—the poet who is driven to madness or death by the disdain of his beloved. Stanislav Zimic suggests the interesting possibility that, in Sosa Coitiño's sudden appearance, brief lament, and unexpected death, Cervantes is satirizing the techniques of character presentation of the *novela bizantina* (see "El *Persiles* como crítica de la novela bizantina," *Acta Neophilologica*, 3 [1970], 49-64). Sosa Coitiño's function in the symbolic movement of the romance is limited to the plane of the main plot; hence I do not treat him below among the figures whose quests constitute analogues of the protagonists' quest.

steer toward a huge mountain. "Con la ayuda del cielo" they reach it, and, on learning that they are in Golandia, a "land of Catholics," they rejoice over their deliverance. As I have pointed out above, Cervantes allows his interest in marvelous descriptions and erudite and moralizing subject matter to dominate in the scenes in Golandia. However, in the adventures which follow the pilgrims' respite we observe a return of the symbolic methods of opening scenes, as the apocalyptic order is closely involved in the events of the narration. During a serene, starry night on a calm sea, Rutilio sings a sonnet evoking the biblical flood and the ark of Noah overcoming death and bearing those who are destined to preserve the human race safely over the waters of purgation (p. 132). As in the description of the vision of Rome, Cervantes here employs a poem recited by a character to establish an imaginative linkage between the heroes' experiences and corresponding moments in biblical history. And, as in Coitiño's sonnet celebrating the ethical values on which the *Persiles* is built, the elements accompany the singer harmoniously.

> ... quedó el navío lleno de muy sosegado silencio, en el cual Rutilio, que iba sentado al pie del árbol mayor, convidado de la serenidad de la noche, de la comodidad del tiempo, o de la voz, que la tenía estremada, al son del viento, que dulcemente hería en las velas, en su propia lengua toscana, comenzó a cantar.
>
> (p. 132)

The song of peace, concord, and rebirth marks the conclusion of the period of deliverance begun with Sosa Coitiño's song and continued in the feasts celebrating the return of the pilgrims to civilization in Golandia. The sage

Mauricio describes his nightmare vision of a cosmic disaster in which their vessel is shattered by bolts of lightning and engulfed in mountainous seas. Shortly thereafter, the ship is scuttled by two soldiers, who confess their desire to abduct Auristela and Transila before perishing in the rising waters. Escaping in two life boats, the heroes find themselves again separated and menaced by the natural forces, which again become destructive and frightening. The night ceases to be benign: the darkness is more impenetrable than before, the stars are less visible, and the weather begins to threaten. The shipwrecked pilgrims spend another long and sleepless night in fear and discover with the daylight their absolute isolation. They reach an island only to find its surface entirely covered with snow which is as hard as stone. The motif of "near-death" reappears in Antonio's despairing words, "¡Mira el poco lugar que nos queda desde este punto al de la muerte" (p. 142). Observing the "imposibilidad y soledad de la isla," the wanderers raise their hands to heaven in silent supplication, repeating the gestures of Periandro and Cloelia in the opening scenes. Once again the note of death sounds at this moment of "near-death" in the fortunes of the heroes. A ship appears, and two gentlemen and a sick woman put ashore on the island; the men fight a duel, wound each other mortally, and, following their death, the woman, who turns out to be Taurisa, the former servant of Auristela, dies. Her death provokes a fit of despair in the heroine, in which she expresses the desire for death and questions God's Providence: "¿Qué red barredera es ésta con que cogen los cielos todos los caminos de mi descanso?" (p. 145).

Following the Catholic burial of Taurisa in the ice, the

pilgrims are delivered from what seems to be certain death by the ship which Sinforosa has sent in search of Periandro. After they have sailed undisturbed in their course for three months, a storm suddenly arises and threatens the heroes with death: "Esperaban la muerte cerrados los ojos, o por mejor decir, la temían sin verla: que la figura de la muerte, en cualquier traje que venga, es espantosa" (p. 160). The familiar motifs reappear. In the power of the elements the ship becomes a scene of confusion: "Todo era confusión, todo era grita, todo suspiros, y todo plegarias" (p. 161). The "mar insolente" tosses the helpless ship throughout a night which is lengthened by the darkness of the following day: ". . . al parecer del día, si se puede llamar día el que no trae consigo claridad alguna" (p. 161). If the endless night recalls the night following the fire on the island of the barbarians and the night of the Apocalypse, Cervantes links the ship back to the cavern-dungeon of Periandro, employing again the image of the grave ("hecha sepultura de cuantos en ella estaban"). The "near-death" motif rises in a crescendo in the narrator's lengthy apostrophe underscoring the unexpected turn in the fortunes of the protagonists and the sepulchral transfiguration of the ship and climaxes in his abrupt statement: ". . . quedaron los muertos sepultados sin tierra." Following its conclusion, the motif of deliverance sounds immediately: ". . . pero los piadosos cielos, que de muy atrás toman la corriente de remediar nuestras desventuras . . ." Heaven calms the elements, the sea becomes once again benign, its waves "mansas y recogidas" and its waters "claros espejos," and the capsized vessel drifts ashore on the island of King Policarpo. Cervantes' literarily self-conscious narrator assures us that the de-

liverance of the wanderers from their tomb is not a
miracle but one of the many mysteries of the world which
do not occur outside the boundaries set by the laws of
nature.[2] Nevertheless, through various allusions, he links
the events to the biblical descent of Jonah into the darkness
of the demonic monster, the leviathan. Through metaphor
the hull of the ship becomes a belly capable of disgorging
what it contains through a mouth. As they emerge, its victims are described as "personas que segunda vez nacieron
al mundo" and "resucitados." Their first gesture repeats the
archetypal gesture which accompanied Periandro's rebirth
from the cavern-sepulcher of the opening scene: "limpiáronse los rostros" (p. 164). The archetypal light-

[2] Here we observe one of the many examples of the tension which
arises when the arbitrary causation demanded by the symbolic
movement of the work threatens to conflict with Cervantes' major
aesthetic concern, plausibility, or the "legitimate marvelous." An
old man appears to offer an account of a similar occurrence in
Genoa, where a capsized ship incredibly drifted into the harbor
and deposited its crew safely ashore. In his emphatic conclusion
Cervantes offers an authorization for the verisimilitude of the
scene: "Yo vi esto, y está escrito este caso en muchas historias
españolas, y aun podría ser viviesen agora las personas que segunda
vez nacieron al mundo del vientre desta galera; y si aquí sucediese
lo mismo, no se ha de tener a milagro, sino a misterio: que los
milagros suceden fuera del orden de la naturaleza, y los misterios
son aquellos que parecen milagros y no lo son, sino casos que acon-
tecen raras veces" (pp. 163-164). What is curious here is that this
statement, which Cervantes inserts to answer the potential criticism
that the Canon of Toledo and the Aristotelians had directed against
the romances, that of their inverisimilitude, while guaranteeing the
mimetic foundation of the scene, at the same time introduces
through metaphor the leviathan myth, which lies behind the
entire incident.

darkness motifs appear as the deliverers are described offering light to those whom they bear from the hull.[3]

Following the deliverance of Auristela from the capsized ship and her reunion with Periandro in the island kingdom of Ybernia, the heroes suddenly find themselves enmeshed in a complicated web of palace intrigues. Here their antagonist is the aged King Policarpo, in whom the beauty of Auristela kindles the flames of an uncontrollable passion. The widowed father of two princesses recognizes that his desires dishonor him: ". . . se ha turbado el curso de mi buena vida, y finalmente, he caído desde la cumbre de mi presunción discreta hasta el abismo bajo de no sé qué deseos" (p. 179). Christian overtones of the allusion to the fall are reinforced as the helpless old man resorts to the evil counsels of Zenotia, an Arab witch who has fled the Spanish Inquisition and boasts that she can summon to the earth the cosmic darkness and disorder of the elemental chaos. In Policarpo's acceptance of her suggestion that he refuse to allow the heroes to leave his kingdom and continue their journey, there is an implication of a surrender to demonic forces: ". . . la rabia de la endemoniada enfermedad de los celos se le apoderó del alma" (p. 220). The climax of this episode, in which the heroes are once again

[3] Cervantes' introduction of the fisherman metaphor to describe the deliverers in their task of listening for heartbeats in the pile of cadavers in the ship and separating the "muertos muertos" from the "vivos que lo parecían" is possibly a coherent element in the biblical mythic pattern visible in the background of the scene—the apostles are fishermen, and their mission is to the save the victims of the sea and the leviathan (see Frye, *Anatomy of Criticism*, pp. 189-192).

held in bondage in an environment of sterility,[4] is the scene of confusion in which Policarpo sets the palace afire and attempts to abduct Auristela. Ironically, the fire, which is intended to further the evil plot, becomes the instrument of salvation for the pilgrims, distracting their adversaries while they make their escape and unmasking the intentions of Policarpo to his countrymen, who immediately depose him and hang his diabolical accomplice Zenotia. In this scene of catastrophe we observe a repetition of the familiar motifs: night, confusion, fear, and a traditional cosmic disaster, in this case the archetypal fire, purging the forces of evil and allowing the chosen to continue in their quest.[5]

[4] In the courtly environment of this adventure it is not a landscape which symbolizes sterility, as in the preceding adventures, but rather the aged, widowed king and his two unwed daughters. In their symbolic function they recall the "urban" symbols of sterility in the *Gitanilla*, the aged squire and his feminine society.

[5] That the fire here does not have true cosmic proportions and does not directly menace the heroes and destroy the antagonists as it does in the climactic scene of the island of the barbarians, simply means that the degree of displacement of the apocalyptic order is here greater than before. The purgation which it effects is symbolically stated as the narrator describes Policarpo's being consumed by the inner fire of his passion as he stands in the midst of his blazing palace. Here he becomes the fire through which the heroes must once again pass on the way to their climactic vision and the fire destroying the demonic antagonist of the elect. Various details indicate that Cervantes modeled the Policarpo incident on the Dido episode of the *Aeneid*. In this climactic scene the link to Virgil's work is most direct, as Cervantes describes Sinforosa in her tower as a "nueva Dido" and the fleeing Periandro, as "otro fugitivo Eneas." As in most other cases in the *Persiles*, the literary eclecticism is meaningful in relation to theme. Cervantes deliberate-

Following the escape, the fugitives thank God for their deliverance, and the familiar motifs of the moment of restoration begin to appear. Darkness gives way to light, the sea is gentle, a favorable wind bears the pilgrims on their course, and they are freed from fear ("no les sobresaltaba ningún recelo ni miedo de ningún suceso adverso" [p. 252]). They arrive at the Island of the Hermits, from which a lighthouse sends forth its beams offering refuge

---

ly maintains two great myths in the background of the scene: the biblical quest of mankind for redemption and salvation and the quest of Aeneas to found the new Troy, Rome. Although the medieval Christian interpretation of the *Aeneid* (i.e., the establishment of the Roman peace, during which the Redeemer would appear, and the city of Rome as the center of the world and the custodian of the Redeemer's Word) undoubtedly survived in the Renaissance, the myth of Aeneas remained basically secular in Cervantes' age. The Trojan hero was the example of unswaying dedication to his duty to found the state and the empire. (El Pinciano claims that the teaching of political wisdom was the principal intention of Virgil and Homer [op. cit., I, 216-217].) The goal of Periandro's quest is, in keeping with tridentine Catholicism, both secular and religious. The heroes' arrival in Rome is to be followed by their return to perfect their kingdom and conceive children. Despite Pfandl's disappointment, it is significant that the vision of earthly perfection which Cervantes projects into the *Persiles* is not the cloister, but rather the city. At two points in the work the ascetic religious solution, i.e., flight from the world, the natural cycle, and temporality, is proposed and rejected. The perfected society and fulfillment of one's duty within it were conceived as part of God's desired order. Significantly Cervantes returns to the myth of Aeneas as the pilgrims arrive in the Eternal City. Impressed by Auristela's beauty, a bystander cries out that Venus has returned to the city to do homage to the relics of her son (p. 428). The allusion is brief, and the context is humorous, but the serious implications of the myth remain.

to the shipwrecked and the weary. While they are gathered around a fire preparing to spend a night "sin pesadumbre alguna" (p. 254), Renato and Eusebia appear and offer them "luz y lumbre" and food in their hermitage atop the mountain of the island. The landscape of the island, which the pilgrims observe on the following day, is the counterweight to all the demonic landscapes of the *Persiles*—the rugged island of the barbarians, the sterile islands of ice, and the false paradises of the sorceress of Periandro's dream and Hipólita (see below). It is the true earthly paradise, the image of the traditional celestial paradise, which will be introduced into the *Persiles* directly in Feliciana de la Voz's song to the Virgin of Guadalupe. The life-giving waters ("puras y limpias") of its numerous streams, which nourish its fruit trees and grass, image the waters of baptism, and the pleasures with which it rewards the wanderers image the delights of the Blessed. The island is the setting for the climax of the series of visionary moments of the northern adventures, which begins with Periandro's gaze toward heaven in the opening scene of the work. The pilgrims enter the hermitage, discover an altar with the illuminated images of Christ, the Virgin, and St. John the Divine, and kneel in prayer.

It is significant that the first half of the *Persiles* concludes with this adventure, for it prefigures the pilgrims' attainment of the ultimate goal of their quest. The hilltop on which they are received by the hermits points toward the hill from which they contemplate the city of Rome in adoration. The altar and prayer anticipate the churches of St. Peter and St. Paul and the instruction of Auristela among the penitentiaries in Rome, and the earthly paradise with its brooks and fruits points toward the city of Rome, itself the image of the apocalyptic city and its fruit-bearing tree and waters of life. The transfiguration of the destructive water of the sea into the life-giving waters of Renato's brooks is equally significant, for at this point the pilgrims will abandon the sea and continue their journey on land.

We might say that the basic key of the *Persiles* which sounds through all the cycles of death and deliverance of the first part is minor. The dominant motifs are darkness, winter, sterility, and death. All of these have given way to light, but the light is always distant and ephemeral. The pilgrims remain at the mercy of the elements, and in the background there is always the frightening specter of the sea. In spite of the fact that the symbolic rhythm of the work dictates the occasional appearance of the sea as a benign force, i.e., in the moments of deliverance,[6] it is generally symbolic of the demonic powers of destruction and death which menace the pilgrims and of the mutability that marks the fallen condition of man in earthly life:[7] (". . . la inconstancia de nuestras vidas y la del mar

---

[6] The most extensive transformation of the sea is in its last appearance in the work: ". . . iban rompiendo, como digo, no claros cristales, sino azules; mostrábase el mar colchado, porque el viento, tratándole con respeto, no se atrevía a tocarle a más de la superficie, y la nave suavemente le besaba los labios, y se dejaba resbalar por él con tanta ligereza, que apenas parecía que le tocaba" (p. 276). Here the element participates in the joyous deliverance of the heroes and prefigures their triumphant entry into the world of civilization at Lisbon.

[7] This is in fact the traditional association of the sea archetype in literature. Discussing the archetypal motifs which characterize the comic and the tragic visions, Frye writes: "In the comic vision the *unformed* world is a river, traditionally fourfold. . . . In the

74

simbolizan en no prometer seguridad ni firmeza alguna largo tiempo" [p. 253], ". . . la segunda tabla de nuestro naufragio, que es la penitencia, sin la cual no hay abrir la senda del cielo" [p. 436], and "la instabilidad del mar" [p. 107]). It is with joy that the pilgrims step onto the shore of the Isle of the Hermits to spend a night "libres de los vaivenes del mar" (p. 253).

The arrival in Portugal, which begins the second half of the *Persiles*, is heralded by the cry of the lookout, which brings an apocalyptic note once again into the narration, as it announces the overcoming of the sea: "¡Tierra! ¡Tierra! Aunque mejor diría: ¡cielo! ¡cielo!"[8] The narrator writes that the city of Lisbon appears to the pilgrims as "la tierra de promisión"; Antonio describes the many temples of the city in which God is worshiped (his words

---

tragic vision this world usually becomes the sea, as the narrative myth of dissolution is so often a flood myth. The combination of the sea and the beast images gives us the leviathan and similar water-monsters," *Fables of Identity* (New York, 1963), p. 20. The Christian mythology of course encompasses both, as the streams of Paradise and the waters of baptism are juxtaposed to the waters of the flood and the haunt of the leviathan. In the *Persiles* the water of Renato's springs and the sea, which creates a "ship-leviathan" swallowing the wanderers, represent these two archetypes.

[8] As in the opening scenes of the work and in those describing the ship-leviathan and Renato's hermitage, here the apocalyptic order is very close to the surface of the *Persiles*. St. John the Divine, whom Cervantes describes as the one "que vio más estando durmiendo, que vieron cuantos ojos tiene el cielo en sus estrellas" (p. 259), describes the New Jerusalem: "Then I saw a new heaven and a new earth; for the first heaven and the first earth had passed away, and the sea was no more. And I saw the holy city, new Jerusalem, coming down out of heaven from God. . ." (Rev., 21:1).

75

"notarás cómo la caridad cristiana está en su punto" [p. 277] are a counterweight to the narrator's statement that in the northern countries "la verdadera fe católica no está en el punto tan perfecto como se requiere" [p. 432]); and Auristela joyously contemplates the emergence of the pilgrims from the sea: "Contentísima estaba Auristela de ver que se le acercaba la hora de poner pie en tierra firme, sin andar de puerto en puerto y de isla en isla, sujeta a la inconstancia del mar y a la movible voluntad de los vientos; y más cuando supo que desde allí a Roma podía ir a pie enjuto sin embarcarse otra vez si no quisiese" (p. 278).

Auristela's fear of the sea lingers throughout her pilgrimage. When Ambrosia Augustina offers to send her and her companions to Rome from Barcelona in her brother's ship, she rejects the offer "escarmentada con tantas esperiencias como había hecho de las borrascas del mar" (p. 366). It is this fear of the sea which causes Auristela to waver in her determination to continue her quest even at the moment when its goal has been attained. Before entering Rome she despairingly reveals to Periandro her fears about the perils of the return journey to their distant kingdom (p. 414). And following her instruction in the Catholic faith, she determines to withdraw to the contemplative life, abandoning "los caminos torcidos y las dudosas sendas" (p. 461) in favor of the "atajos llanos," claiming that she wants to go to heaven "sin rodeos, sin sobresaltos, y sin cuidados" (p. 459). Her desire is to escape the sea and the cycle of "trabajos" which it represents. Auristela's ascetic solution is clearly a false one: the ultimate meaning of the *Persiles* is the acceptance of man's duty to participate in the life cycle, to make his way through the dark labyrinths of human history, and with the aid of faith and revelation discover the light that is ever partially obscured.

PERIANDRO'S RECITATION

In its composition, Book II is the most complicated part of the *Persiles* and the part in which Cervantes' preoccupations with the literary reality of his work are most acute. It is here that our patience with the entanglements of Cervantes' narrative threads is most strained. In the foreground we must follow a series of intrigues which develop simultaneously. Sinforosa confides in Auristela, hoping to wed Periandro; Clodio and Rutilio conspire in the hope of possessing Auristela and Policarpa; the witch Zenotia desires the embraces of the youthful Antonio and punishes his resistance by inflicting a deadly illness upon him; King Policarpo solicits Sinforosa's help and conspires with Zenotia to possess Auristela. While developing these intrigues simultaneously by shifting rapidly from one narrative fragment to another, Cervantes increases the complication by projecting a second and entirely different plane of narration. In Periandro's recitation, a series of fragments interspersed amid the unfolding drama, we witness several of the events which preceded the hero's imprisonment in the dungeon of the barbarians, where we find him in the opening scene of the work.

In another study I have shown how Periandro's recitation is almost exclusively the product of Cervantes' interest in literary problems and reveals clearly his ambivalent attitude toward the neoclassical theories which lay behind his conception of the *Persiles*. On the one hand, the recitation represents his clearest tribute to the theorists and the classical models. As El Pinciano pointed out repeatedly, the excellence of the well-constructed epic is dependent to a great extent on the *in-medias-res* beginning and the subsequent exposition of the events preceding the beginning. Homer in the *Odyssey* and Virgil in the *Aeneid* successfully exploited the technique, and Heliodorus perfected it by delaying the necessary exposition until the midpoint of his *Aethiopica*. Periandro's recitation is what El Pinciano calls the "delayed prologue" of heroic poems and corresponds to the recitations of Odysseus, Aeneas, and Calasiris in the ancient epics. The hero's occasional allusions to the process of catching up narrative threads, as well as the praise which his audience accords his way of linking events, allow us to glimpse Cervantes' awareness of the contemporary theoretical interest surrounding the disposition of the epic. Moreover, if Periandro's role as narrator recalls that of his classical ancestors, his adventures are rich in reminiscences of classical literature. The boat race on the island of the fishermen is closely modeled on the festivities at Anchises' grave in the *Aeneid*; in the background of his visit to the island paradise are both Circe and the Sirens; like Palinurus he gazes at the stars while at the helm; like Odysseus he must contend with a seamonster which swallows sailors; his encounter with Sulpicia recalls such classical warrior maidens as Pentasilea and Camila, as well as their Renaissance descendants; and his horse-breaking in the kingdom of King Cratilo of Lithuania is reminiscent of the famous scene of Alexander and Bucephelas. The imitation of such classical models was perfectly in keeping with contemporary theories of literature, and Cervantes undoubtedly composed his scenes thinking that they would add luster and prestige to his prose epic.[9]

At the same time, it is important to observe that in composing several of the scenes in Periandro's narration, Cervantes uses literature and literary history to examine critically certain theories of the neoclassical school which he held to be restrictive on creative activity—namely, its scrupulous prohibition of any episode not subordinated to and integrated in the plot of the epic poem and its empirically oriented interpretation of the Aristotelian principle of mimesis. Cervantes embodies these theories in a critical audience which punctuates Periandro's recitation with praise and censure of his narrative procedures. Thus we could speak of a third narrative plane which Cervantes projects into this most complicated interlude of the *Persiles*, one in which we observe in brief fragments the development of a dramatic encounter between the creating artist and the literary theorist. The adventure of the fishermen's wedding examines unity; that of the island paradise examines both unity and verisimilitude; and that of Periandro's leap on King Cratilo's horse examines verisimilitude.[10]

Returning to the question of the structure of the *Persiles*, I regard the series of adventures narrated by

[9] For Cervantes' theories concerning the imitation of classical models, see Riley, pp. 61-67.

[10] See my *Cervantes, Aristotle, and the "Persiles,"* Chs. VI-VII. Zimic ("El *Persiles* como crítica de la novela bizantina") observes the importance of literary problems in these scenes and argues that at this point Cervantes cannot resist criticizing some of the basic conventions of the romances which he is in fact imitating in the *Persiles*—e.g., innumerable adventures, irrelevant descriptions, and complications of plot.

Periandro to be one of the most marvelous, but least allegorical, interludes of the *Persiles*. Certainly some of them reflect thematically on the ethical problems raised in the intrigues on Policarpo's island and for that matter in the rest of the *Persiles*. The adventure of the fishermen's wedding does indeed examine the nature of perfect love and marriage, which are important themes at various points in the work. The tale of King Leopoldio of Danea, who leaves his state to pursue his faithless wife, can be interpreted ethically as an example of what might ensue when a king marries in his old age and can be related to Policarpo's desire to wed Auristela. Sulpicia as a victim of lust and treachery can be related to all the members of the protagonists' party who are menaced by lustful antagonists. Moreover, as some of the adventures follow the pattern of struggle-bondage-deliverance, it can be argued that the sustained symbolical movement of the work allows us to observe the recurrent cycle which through myth, allusion, and metaphor is generally linked to the Christian vision of man and history. It is certainly valid to observe in the sea of ice, which imprisons Periandro's ship and menaces his crew with starvation, the savage horse which hurls the hero toward certain death on the frozen surface of the sea, and the sea-monster of the northern waters, the "náufrago," which swallows one of his crewmen, more of the demonic places and antagonists which attempt to thwart the providential plan. However, in these scenes the emphasis is on the "glittering surface of adventure" and suspense (the water freezing around the boat, the marvelous spectacle of an endless expanse of ice, the inhabitants of Danea skating across its surface, all wonders verified by contemporary scholarship on the northern lands) and ornamental description (the resplendent armor of the warrior-maiden Sulpicia, the scintillating garden of the sorceress). The "náufrago" itself, the water-spewing sea-monster which devours one of the elect, is far less a reactualization of the leviathan than is the ship of Policarpo, which, storm-tossed in the lengthened night of the Apocalypse, capsizes and imprisons the elect in its belly. Here there are no allusions or metaphors to thrust the Christian myth into the foreground and interpose a layer of conceptual meaning between the reader and the adventures of the narration.[11]

Of all the adventures in Periandro's recitation, the most important is his visit to the island paradise, which, as the reader and the hero's spellbound audience discover at its conclusion, is in reality a dream vision. In it we observe a fusion of adventure, embellishing ornament, and literary theme, characteristic of the rest of the recitation, with the symbolic movement which otherwise is dominant in the romance. In fact it is the only purely symbolical episode of the work, as Cervantes presents the vision of bondage and deliverance, fall and resurrection, in an encounter between Periandro and allegorical personages. The setting of the dream vision is an island in the remote waters of the north.

---

[11] It is of course possible that the "baroque reader" read these scenes primarily for allegorical meaning and not for their marvelous adventures. Casalduero observes in the sea of ice the symbol of man's isolation and his desire for union; in Sulpicia as avenging warrior, a modern Judith, and as an unprotected woman, a temptation which Periandro's heroic chastity must overcome; in the "náufrago" and the horse of King Cratilo, symbols of passion; and in the stars toward which the hero gazes while at the helm, the symbols of the purity toward which he aspires (i.e., the stars of Fray Luis de León). In the absence of concrete support from the text, such interpretations must remain conjectural.

Periandro and his band put ashore in search of supplies and find themselves in a garden paradise where brooks of liquid diamonds flow through fields of emeralds. Fruit-laden trees offer an abundance of cherries, apples, and pears, and the variety of fruits attests to the absence of any seasonal change. The entire scene delights the eye, the soft murmur of the fountains and the song of birds caress the ear, and the fruits regale the other senses with their fragrance, their sweetness, and their delicacy. Amid the enumeration of such traditional features of the garden paradise, a sinister note sounds. Intermingled with the fruits are jewels which resemble them so perfectly that the visitors cannot distinguish rubies from cherries. The birds, whose song is so pleasing, are in reality captives (". . . parecía que en aquel distrito tenían cautiva su libertad y que no querían ni acertaban a cobrarla" [p. 242]). Appearances can deceive: sensuous enjoyment can enslave. At this point a procession emerges from the narrow opening of a cliff—twelve stout apes ("animales lascivos"), a carriage in the form of a battered ship, a beautiful woman with a staff, and behind her a band of attendants playing various musical instruments. The sorceress, whose staff bears an escutcheon with the word "Sensuality," threatens Periandro, whom she addresses as her enemy; her attendants snatch up seven or eight of his men, who are paralyzed by the music; and the whole procession disappears into the mountain. The pilgrims now hear a sweeter music and witness a second procession, a group of singing maidens led by the goddess Chastity, who appears in the form of Auristela, and her two attendants, Continence and Modesty. They assure Periandro that they will protect

Auristela "hasta que con dichoso fin le dé a sus trabajos y peregrinaciones en la alma ciudad de Roma" (p. 243).

The form of this episode is strikingly similar to that of the court masque, which, as Jean Rousset has shown, was one of the most popular literary genres of the age. The momentary triumph of evil followed by the triumph of good, the battle between Sensuality and Chastity, the involvement of supernatural beings and allegorical figures, the processional form and the accompanying music, the figure of the sorceress, the wild animals, the garden paradise, the cliff, the cave, and the audience's involvement in the action are all conventions of this spectacular literary form.[12] The presence of such a form is a good example of how in its eclecticism the *Persiles* assimilates subject matter and forms from a wide variety of literary genres to its underlying theme. In effect, the masque, which as a dream vision is reconcilable with Cervantes' theories of verisimilitude, contains an emblematic statement of the entire *Persiles*: the heroes will suffer many ordeals, but their virtue and perseverance in adversity will eventually triumph, for Providence is guiding them on their pilgrimage.

In the total context of the *Persiles*, Periandro's dream represents one of the visionary moments which mark the heroes' pilgrimage toward Rome. Its demonic cave looks backward to the cave-dungeon of the opening scene and

---

[12] See *La Littérature de l'âge baroque en France* (Paris, 1954), Ch. I. For the fortunes of this type of drama in Spain, see N. D. Shergold, *A History of the Spanish Stage from Medieval Times until the End of the Seventeenth Century* (Oxford, 1967), Chs. IX-XII. For the function of this type of scene in narrative literature of the Renaissance, see A. Bartlett Giamatti, op. cit.

forward to its apocalyptic counterweight, the cave of Soldino in Book III. Its demonic gardens look backward to the demonic islands of ice and rock, as well as to their apocalyptic counterweight, the circular verdant area near Antonio's cavern-refuge, and forward to the mountain-top garden of the hermits, the celestial paradise of Feliciana's song, and the garden of Soldino, as well as to the demonic false paradise of the courtesan Hipólita in Rome. The demonic monsters, the apes, look backward to the wolves, the sea-monster, and the ship-leviathan and forward to the infernal serpent of Feliciana's song and the dragon associated with Ruperta. The demonic music which enslaves recalls the music of the barbarians, which filled the air with "confusos y diferentes sones"; the divine music of Chastity's procession recalls Rutilio's song about the great flood and looks forward to Feliciana's hymn to the Virgin and the harmonious music which the pilgrims hear in Toledo.

THE SOUTHERN ADVENTURES: TOWARD A TONE OF COMEDY

In keeping with the symbolic movement of the *Persiles*, we observe a modulation from despair to festivity in the general tonality of its final two books. The ephemeral light which the pilgrims glimpse occasionally in the gloomy reaches of the north now illuminates the entire landscape. The sea is replaced by land; a sterile nature, by a bountiful nature; darkness, by light; winter, by spring and summer; bondage, by deliverance; fear, by confidence; isolation, by marriage; and the tragic moment of the Christian cycle, by the comic. While the lonely, isolated figure and the remote island are typical of the first part of the *Persiles*, the triumphant reintegration of the wanderers into society and the temple (Lisbon, Guadalupe, Talavera, Toledo, Monserrate, Rome) dominate throughout the second part. The experience of hell is abbreviated; the experience of heaven is prolonged.

As the pilgrims disembark in Lisbon, the dwellers of the city pour from their houses to admire their beauty ("Había salido a la marina infinita gente a ver los estranjeros desembarcados en Belén; corrieron allá todos por ver la novedad, que siempre se lleva tras sí los deseos y los ojos" [pp. 278-279]). Indeed the wanderers form a spectacle for the pleasure of the surrounding world ("... causaban espanto y maravilla a quien los miraba ... Llegaron por tierra a Lisboa, rodeados de plebeya y de cortesana gente; lleváronlos al gobernador, que, después de admirado de verlos ... la novedad de los [trajes] que traían era la causa principal de ser tan seguidos, que ya parecían perseguidos del vulgo" [p. 279]). This pageantry and universal rejoicing establishes the tone of comedy that predominates throughout the rest of the work, and it is not surprising that, immediately following their departure from Portugal, the pilgrims meet a poet who proposes to turn their adventures into a comedy. The motif of spectacle[13] is resumed at the goal of the heroes' quest, as they are surrounded in Rome

[13] The germ of such scenes of spectacle and celebration can be observed in the deliverance of the pilgrims in Golandia (p. 106) and Policarpo's kingdom (p. 165). However, the significant difference is the brevity of such scenes in the northern adventures and their failure to establish a tone. Similarly the distant light amid darkness of the northern landscape anticipates the sunlight of the south; yet light is dominant over darkness only in the second part of the work. As I have pointed out, both moments of the cycle are present in each adventure. It is the emphasis that varies.

by a clamorous throng which celebrates the beauty of Auristela. Moreover, some of the episodes of this part are animated by the spirit of comedy, presenting the triumph of a comic society over forces of unnatural laws obstructing its wishes, and depicting the celebration of its victory by multitudes. These celebrations include such traditional conclusions of comedy as a banquet, a community dance, and various weddings.[14]

In spite of the dominance of a tone of comedy in the second half of the *Persiles*, the cyclical rhythm of death and deliverance continues in the series of adventures engaging the pilgrims on their road toward the climactic vision of Rome. The first of the "near-deaths" of the wanderers in the civilized world is the brief prison scene, which has been examined above in connection with Cervantes' technique of fragmentary narration. Following their release, the cycle quickly takes its turn, and they experience one of the most important visions of the work. On entering the valley of Guadalupe they look upward in wonder to the towering peaks and "el grande y suntuoso monasterio, cuyas murallas encierran la santísima imagen de la emperadora de los cielos; la santísima imagen, otra vez, que es libertad de los cautivos, lima de sus hierros y alivio de sus pasiones; la santísima imagen que es salud de las enfermedades, consuelo de los afligidos, madre de los huérfanos y reparo de las desgracias" (p. 305). As they enter the shrine, they behold everywhere relics which speak of suffering and regeneration, death and resurrection, the pattern repeatedly actualized in the narration of the *Persiles*: abandoned crutches, eyes of wax, artificial limbs, and "mortajas de que se desnudaron los muertos,

[14] See Frye, *Anatomy of Criticism*, pp. 163-164.

todos después de haber caído en el suelo de las miserias, ya vivos, ya sanos, ya libres y ya contentos, merced a la larga misericordia de la Madre de las misericordias, que en aquel pequeño lugar hace campear a su benditísimo Hijo con el escuadrón de sus infinitas misericordias." Moved deeply by the spectacle, the pilgrims seem to see throngs of sufferers flying through the air to find salvation in the temple, and in astonishment they kneel in prayer.

At this moment of intense worship the maiden Feliciana, whose voice is as sweet as that of "algún ángel de los confirmados en gracia," sings a hymn to the Virgin. The song alludes briefly to the elemental chaos before the creation and the ordering of the movements of the spheres and then turns to its central event, the conception of the Virgin by God. It ends on a prophetic note, describing the moment in history when the angel Gabriel is preparing to make his holy embassy, the Annunciation. Feliciana imaginatively identifies the City of God (i.e., the heavenly bride of the Apocalypse) with the theological and cardinal virtues and the Virgin, and describes her conception as the construction of a celestial palace whose pillars rise through the four elements and soar beyond the circle of the moon and which is surrounded by gardens, orchards, inexhaustible fountains, flowers, fruits, and trees (pp. 309-311). This is, of course, the traditional celestial paradise (i.e., Revelation; Dante, *Paradiso*, xxx), which is the true destination of all the wanderers who fill the pages of the *Persiles*. Employing a series of apocalyptic images, Feliciana heralds the imminent overcoming of the "sombras tenebrosas del pecado," the "cadena del hierro antiguo," the "infernal serpiente," and the garments of mourning which mankind has worn since the fall and announces the restoration of the "dawn" (the Virgin), the "light of the sun" (Christ), and the "venidero Agosto" (the regeneration of man).

Although focused on the Immaculate Conception and the birth of Christ, the hymn of Feliciana de la Voz, through a rich concentration of biblical allusions and imagery reaching from Genesis to Revelation, can be said to span the entirety of history. The celestial palace with its gardens is simultaneously Eden, the imperfect temple of Solomon, and the New Jerusalem. Christ is both the lamb of God, the "true sacrifice," prefigured imperfectly in Abraham's sacrifice of Isaac, and the Messiah of the Apocalypse. The serpent is both the corrupter of Adam and the dragon slain by the Messiah. It is significant that at this point the verses are "mas estimados que entendidos" by Auristela, who can comprehend the meaning of history and the mystery that human life continually reenacts only after her instruction among the penitentiaries in Rome.

In its introduction of the divine order into the context of the *Persiles*, the hymn is the most important of the various allusions and symbols by which Cervantes links the Christian myth with the cycle of fall and restoration in the quests of his characters. Placed at the center of the *Persiles*, the moment when the protagonists have left behind the darkness of the north and the perils of the sea (linked in the song with "la borrasca antigua"), it effectively associates that moment with the midpoint of history, the birth of Christ, and strengthens the various associations of the ordeals of the northern world with those suffered by God's chosen people in the Old Testament. It is not surprising that in their next ordeal, the protagonists are associated with Christ's betrayal in Jerusalem, and,

when we discover toward the end of the *Persiles* the sonnet associating Rome with the New Jerusalem, we must
look back to the sonnet on the great flood near the beginning and the hymn to the Virgin at the middle and recognize that there is definitely a biblical shape in Cervantes'
final work.

If Feliciana de la Voz's hymn allows us to glimpse in an
undisplaced form the mythic order which the *Persiles*, in
both its totality and its individual units, reactualizes, the
succeeding visionary moment returns to the less allegorical
methods characteristic of most of the work. The protagonists enter Toledo, which as the historical setting for both
the captivity and liberation of God's elect, is a suitable
analogue of Rome and Jerusalem. In a scene which prefigures the adoration of Rome from the hill and the words
of the sonnet associating it with the Heavenly City, Periandro contemplates Toledo and the "celebrated" Tagus,
addresses words of reverence to the river, and then
offers his homage to the city: "¡Oh peñascosa pesadumbre,
gloria de España y luz de sus ciudades, en cuyo seno han
estado guardadas por infinitos siglos las reliquias de los
valientes godos, para volver a resucitar su muerta gloria, y
a ser claro espejo y depósito de católicas ceremonias! ¡Sal-
ve, pues, oh ciudad santa, y da lugar que en ti le tengan
estos que venimos a verte!" (p. 327)

In the succeeding description of the festival in Toledo
and the gardens in Aranjuez we observe a complete in-
version of the demonic social and elemental worlds depicted in the northern adventures. The lust and sodomy
of the northern societies are here replaced by married love
and its offspring; the fear, mistrust, and greed which hold
the society of the barbarians together are replaced by forth-

rightness, justice, and Christian mercy; the tendency to disintegration which distinguishes the societies of Policarpo and the barbarians is replaced by the orderly movement of the community dances; the "confusos y diferentes sones" of the barbarians' music and the "cabriola" of their dance are replaced by the consonances of the peasants' musical instruments and the intricacies of their dance.

What Cervantes describes in Toledo is a spectacle of earthly harmony which reflects the harmony of the universe and the Heavenly Kingdom. The joyous sound of an infinite number of musical instruments fills the valleys surrounding the city, and beautiful young peasants in colorful attire form several groups, each constituted by a nucleus of maidens with an outer circle of youths revolving about it. All the dancers "componían un honesto movimiento, aunque de diferentes bailes formado." The infinite number of instruments blend so that "de todos estos sones redundaba uno solo, que alegraba con la concordancia, que es el fin de la música" (p. 328). Even if Feliciana's poem had not just alluded to the motion of the spheres and their song, it would not be overinterpreting to find in the movements of the dances and the harmonies of the song a reflection of the cosmic harmonies. To read this scene as an example of Cervantes' mastery of local color in the "realistic" half of the *Persiles*, as is commonly done, is to impoverish it immeasurably.

At this point the function of the allusion to the Latin language at the beginning of the chapter is clear. It is not made merely to render Periandro's startling knowledge of Garcilaso de la Vega's works plausible. Here the linguistic fragmentation of the northern world (Lithua-

nian, Polish, English, the brutish tones of the barbarians),
which recalls the confusion of Babel and images the tendency toward disintegration marking the fallen world
of temporality, is overcome. Latin is the language of a
redeemed humanity united under the Church and the
image of the song of the Heavenly Society. If the language, music, and dance of the social world suggest a
unified variety, the natural world reveals the same characteristic. In the gardens of Aranjuez, an earthly analogue
of the celestial paradise of Feliciana's song and the counterweight to the northern islands of ice, the pilgrims discover an abundance of fruits and a diversity of flowers all
united in an astonishing concert and behold "la junta, los
besos y abrazos que se daban los dos famosos ríos Henares
y Tajo."

The view of beauty as a proportionate interrelationship
of parts and whole appears elsewhere in Cervantes'
works,[15] but never with such cosmic implications and
with the richness and density of expression marking this
episode of the *Persiles*. Music, the dance, the garden, the
Latin language, which unites different nationalities, all
reveal the beauty of unity in variety. Moreover, Cervantes
here speaks of beauty itself as if it were a composition of

---

[15] In the *Galatea* Lenio speaks of corporeal beauty in terms of
the concept: ". . . ésta consiste en que todas las partes del cuerpo
sean de por sí buenas, y que todas juntas hagan un todo perfecto y
formen un cuerpo proporcionado de miembros y suavidad de
colores" (ed. cit., II, 44). Discussing the construction of a work
of fiction, the Canon of Toledo introduces the idea in a criticism
of the flawed plots of the romances of chivalry: "No he visto
ningún libro de caballerías que haga un cuerpo de fábula entero
con todos sus miembros, de manera que el medio corresponda al
principio, y el fin al principio y al medio" (I, 482).

parts: ". . . admirados de ver la hermosura de las labradoras doncellas, que parecían, todas a una mano, que eran *principio, medio,* y *fin* de la humana belleza" (p. 330). The vision which animates the entire episode is reflected stylistically in the even rhythms of its prose:

Casi en este mismo instante resonó en sus oídos el son de infinitos y alegres instrumentos que por los valles que la ciudad rodean se estendían, y vieron venir hacia donde ellos estaban escuadrones *no armados de infantería, sino montones de doncellas,* sobre el mismo sol hermosas, *vestidas* a lo villano, *llenas* de *sartas* y *patenas* los pechos, en quien los *corales* y la *plata* tenían su *lugar* y *asiento,* con más gala que *las perlas* y *el oro,* que aquella vez *se hurtó de los pechos y se acogió a los cabellos,* que todos eran *luengos* y *rubios* como el mismo oro; venían, *aunque sueltos por las espaldas, recogidos en la cabeza con verdes guirnaldas de olorosas flores.* Campeó aquel día, y en ellas, antes la palmilla de Cuenca que el damasco de Milán y el raso de Florencia. Finalmente, la rusticidad de sus galas se aventajaba a las más ricas de la corte, porque *si en ellas se mostraba la honesta medianía, se descubría asimismo la estremada limpieza: todas eran flores, todas rosas, todas donaire, y todas juntas* componían un honesto movimiento, aunque de diferentes bailes formado . . . (p. 328).[16]

In its symmetrical arrangement of parallel units and antitheses and its frequent balancing of such units in pairs, the passage is a good example of what Helmut Hatzfeld has called Cervantes' *Schäferstil* and attributed

[16] The italics are mine.

to the influence of the classics on the development of his prose style.[17]

If the bondage of the dungeon-cave on the barbarians' island and the mythic order associated with it are only dimly visible in the pilgrims' first incarceration in the south—which is dominated in fact by elements of social satire and a mysterious love intrigue[18]—their ordeal in the village of the *moriscos* reveals the close presence of demonic and divine agencies in the action which is characteristic of the northern adventures. Antonio's words of astonishment at the unexpected hospitality of the inhabitants and Periandro's reply imaginatively introduce the biblical order as a background for the scene of treachery.

—Yo no sé quién dice mal desta gente, que todos me parecen unos santos.
—Con palmas—dijo Periandro—recibieron al Señor en Jerusalén los mismos que de allí a pocos días le pusieron en una cruz.   (pp. 353-354)

After accepting the hospitality of an old *morisco*, whose generous offer, the narrator assures us, is made "no morisca, sino cristianamente" (p. 354), the pilgrims are informed by their host's daughter Rafala that her father intends to murder them and flee with a fleet of Barbary pirates, with whom he and others in the village have conspired. The biblical overtones that have announced the scene are reinforced in her description of the pilgrims as coming like "mansas y simples ovejas al matadero," her account of the seduction of the villagers by the Turkish pirates, who promise them "el gusto de sus cuerpos y

[17] *"Don Quijote" als Wortkunstwerk* (Leipzig, 1927), pp. 223 ff.
[18] See above, p. 21.

la salvación de sus almas" in the land of Berbería, and in her insistence that the heroes take refuge in the church with the only two "cristianos viejos" of the village (pp. 354-355).

In the church the pilgrims hear a prophecy of an ancient astrologer full of apocalyptic notes, describing the *moriscos* as the "serpent which is gnawing at the entrails of Spain," associating them with vegetable sterility and forces devastating the country ("espinas y malezas que la [tierra] oprimen," "la mala yerba de los sembrados," "la neguilla del trigo" [p. 356]), and stating that the time is nigh for the advent of a deliverer, a king of the house of Austria. The prophecy culminates in an exhortation of the youthful redeemer to come and rid the region of the blighting force so that the "cristianos viejos" can populate the land and restore its fertility. Once again Cervantes assimilates contemporary history to his underlying transcendental theme. As persecutors of the Christian heroes, the enemies of the Spanish state converge imaginatively with the powers of hell, and the salvation of the heroes converges with the destruction of the *moriscos*. By the same token, Philip III, the scourge of the *moriscos*, converges with the divine agencies which deliver the heroes. In this most patriotic interlude of a work whose major theme is universal, Spain momentarily becomes a battleground of apocalyptic forces, and its king becomes analogous to God and Christ.[19]

[19] As the Ricote episode of the *Quixote* indicates, Cervantes' attitude toward Philip III's decision to expel the *moriscos* is much more complicated than this scene would suggest (see Américo Castro's study of the apparent contradictions in Cervantes' treatment of the problem of the *morisco*, *El pensamiento de Cervantes*

Following the prophecy, the pilgrims and the priest ascend to the tower of the church, bearing with them the monstrance and the Blessed Sacrament, and prepare to resist the imminent onslaught. As in previous adventures, we observe at the moment of potential disaster the motifs of darkness, confusion, fire, the sea, and the de-

---

[Madrid, 1925], pp. 292-307). One could perhaps explain the differences between the *Quixote's* and the *Persiles'* presentations of the *morisco* in terms of the differences between the function of character in novel and in romance (see below, Ch. IV, where I pursue this idea in reference to the figures of Hadji Morato in the *Quixote* and Rafala's father in the *Persiles*). Taking a more biographical and sociological approach, one might explain the differences in terms of the two tendencies which Castro maintains mark the activity of the *cristiano nuevo* in Spain of the sixteenth and early seventeenth centuries: "El cristiano nuevo se deshacía interiormente al esforzarse por ser como todos, hacer como todos (ingresar, por ejemplo, en respetables cofradías religiosas), y a la vez por separarse de los más" (*Cervantes y los casticismos españoles*, p. 113). In fact it could be argued that the two tendencies are observable in this patriotic scene of the *Persiles*. For in the prophecy's curious allusion to the saviors of the region as "nuevos cristianos viejos," it would appear that Cervantes cannot resist an ironic thrust at the caste-consciousness of his society (i.e., the "newly arrived" old Christians can be old Christians who are concealing their *converso* ancestry or old Christians who for some reason or other have recently found it necessary to discover and affirm that they are old Christians). Don Quijote certainly speaks for Cervantes when he affirms that "la sangre se hereda, y la virtud se aquista, y la virtud vale por sí sola lo que la sangre no vale" (II, 841), and, as Castro has shown, Cervantes' rejection of his contemporaries' vulgar notions concerning "limpieza de sangre" is evident throughout his works. What is peculiar in the reference in this episode is that the irony at the expense of the "cristianos viejos" accompanies a description of the "cristianos nuevos," the *moriscos*, as a "mala casta" and the association of the latter with the numerous

monic monster. The ships of the Turk, "el enemigo común del género humano" (p. 272), loom out of the darkness, reach the shore, and are welcomed by the treacherous *moriscos*. Amid the deafening pealing of the alarm bells of the entire region, pirates and traitors plunder and burn the village, invoking the name of Mohammed as they destroy a stone image of the Cross. Like the flames that ravaged the island of the barbarians and the palace of Policarpo, the fire is here both the instrument of the demonic antagonists of the pilgrims and the biblical flames of purgation, by which a wrathful God destroys his adversaries.

Beleaguered by the hosts of *moriscos*, who attempt to set the church afire, the small group in the tower prays to God, who is present in the Blessed Sacrament, to deliver

---

diabolical forces opposing the heroes. The clean oppositions running through the romance are momentarily clouded by a seemingly inappropriate bit of social satire. Do we discover in what probably is Cervantes' most conformist work a trace of what Castro has described as "la tensión entre el ánimo aislado de quien escribe y la resistencia ofrecida por la sociedad de los más, entre quien se siente superior y esclarecido, y el vulgo oprimente y amorfo" (p. 85), a trace which the author cannot conceal? It should be emphasized, however, that such criticism of the values of Spanish society, just as the criticism of the ostentatious pilgrim, who seems to reduce her religion to a series of visits to shrines (pp. 312-315), the criticism of contemporary codes of honor in Periandro's advice to Ortel Banedre (pp. 324-326), and the possible criticism of the Inquisition's informers (p. 201; see Castro, *Cervantes y los casticismos españoles*, p. 117), does not in any way contradict the orthodoxy of the vision of man and history, good and evil, celebrated throughout the *Persiles*. "Cervantes se queda con Cristo y con lo realmente dogmático de la fe católica. Lo que no era eso fue, en gran parte, sometido a una crítica muy punzante" (Castro, p. 92).

them and His temple from danger. Deliverance quickly comes, and Cervantes' self-conscious narrator intervenes to inform us that the apparently miraculous deliverance is in fact no miracle at all. In their effect his words recall the anecdote of the old man in the scene of the capsized ship (see above), for they reveal once again Cervantes' concern lest the adventure's rich allusiveness to the apocalyptic order obscure the mimetic movement of his work and offend against the rules prescribed by the contemporary theory of verisimilitude: ". . . lágrimas echaron Auristela y Constanza pidiendo a Dios, que presente tenían, que de tan manifiesto peligro los librase, y ansimismo que no ofendiese el fuego a su templo, el cual no ardió, *no por milagro, sino porque las puertas eran de hierro, y porque fue poco el fuego que se les aplicó*" (p. 358).[20] The light of day returns, revealing that the predatory monster has returned to his haunt at sea, and the group descends from the tower to the altar of the church, where Rafala utters a prayer of thanks to God for their deliverance, and her uncle repeats the call to a young king to uproot the "zarzas, las malezas y las otras yerbas que estorban el crecimiento de la fertilidad y abundancia cristiana" (p. 359).

The rhythm of "near-death" and resurrection continues in the encounter between Periandro and Domicio. A woman falls from a high tower into the group of pilgrims below and is miraculously saved by the braking effect of her billowing skirts. Again the narrator assures us that it is a "cosa posible, sin ser milagro" (p. 373). She beseeches Periandro to save her children and servants from her mad husband, who meanwhile is attempting to hurl

[20] The italics are mine.

97

another woman to earth. Periandro, "impelido de la generosidad de su ánimo" ascends to the tower and struggles with the madman. Once again the adversary is linked with demonic forces, for he has been enslaved by the witchcraft of a jealous woman, who has presented him with a beautiful shirt which has destroyed his sanity. The Hercules myth lies in the background of this adventure, and within the pattern of the struggle of demonic and divine agencies marking so many scenes in the *Persiles*, its presence is sufficient to introduce imaginatively the apocalyptic element of fire and to link Periandro's "near-death" with the death and resurrection of the mythical hero.[21] Periandro and Domicio fall from the tower, and both appear to be dead. Auristela throws herself on her lover, seeking to catch his last breath, and utters a highly rhetorical lament, referring to him as a mountain struck by lightning from heaven. Periandro revives momentarily to say: "yo muero en la fe católica cristiana" (p. 378). This moment of "near-death" is quickly followed by the moment of resurrection. With the aid of the "acostumbrada misericordia de Dios, que mira por los inocentes," Periandro recovers, and the group can continue on its way, leaving behind Claricia

---

[21] The jealous Lorena offers the shirt "como envió la falsa Deyanira la camisa a Hércules." Other elements of the Hercules myth are suggested—the madness of Domicio, his attempt to slay his children, and Auristela's comparison of the fallen Periandro to a mountain destroyed by the thunderbolt. Hercules' apotheosis followed his death in the flames of the shirt and the funeral pyre on the summit of a mountain and the destruction of the pyre by the thunderbolts of Jupiter. In Cervantes' scene the associations of the Hercules myth break down into "positive" and "negative" and are attached to the protagonist and antagonist respectively.

and her children freed from the menaces of the dead Domicio and the demonic forces which enslaved him.

If the moment of potential disaster overshadows that of deliverance in Periandro's struggle with Domicio, in the following adventure the moment of salvation and triumphant vision is dominant. A venerable astrologer with beard and staff enters the inn in which the pilgrims are lodged and announces that a fire will break out in the kitchen and consume the entire building. Like many other prophecies in the *Persiles*, his proves to be correct, and the pilgrims flee the inn to take refuge in his cave. The kitchen fire certainly does not have the proportions of a cosmic disaster, such as we observed in the cataclysmic northern adventures and in the assault of the Barbary pirates. Moreover, there is no explicit association of it with demonic forces and with God's wrath against these forces. Regardless of the predominance of the mimetic factor over the symbolic, this fourth fire of the *Persiles* must be viewed within the broad context of the work as one more potential disaster which the protagonists must overcome[22] and as the necessary prelude, demanded by the logic of the recurrent ritual, to the moment of triumphant vision, which is clearly the moment which Cervantes chooses to emphasize in this adventure. The flight to Soldino's cave-hermitage reenacts the flight to Antonio's hut amid the flames consuming the island of the barbarians, the flight from the burning palace of Policarpo to the Island of the Hermits, and the flight with the Holy Sacrament to the tower of the church to escape

[22] The menacing character of the fire, as well as the "near-death" of the pilgrims, is implicit in the narrator's words: "a cogerles el fuego de noche, fuera milagro escapar alguno que contara su furia" (p. 394).

the fire and sword of the *moriscos* and the invading pirates.

The description of the cave of Soldino as an underground paradise is rich in literary overtones and is linked by the narrator to the aesthetic problems which appear occasionally as themes throughout the *Persiles*, namely the value of imaginative literature, the marvelous, verisimilitude, and artistic freedom.[23] Moreover, Cervantes uses Soldino's account of his life to celebrate the ethical values which had originated in the writings of classical antiquity and had been revived and Christianized by the humanists of the Renaissance. Here we observe the traditional themes of the sixteenth-century reworkings of the Horatian *Beatus ille*: rejection of a corrupt and hypocritical society, retreat to a pleasant and bountiful nature, dedication to the life of solitude and contemplation, all directed toward the attainment of peace and the inner, moral perfection of man (". . . aquí soy yo señor de mí mismo").

Amid the orchestration of classical and secular values in the cave of Soldino, the Christian vision that informs the cyclical rhythm of death and resurrection in the adventures of the *Persiles* persists as an undercurrent. The streams and fruit-bearing trees of his *locus amoenus* are linked imaginatively back through the garden on the Island of the Hermits, through the mountain stream and verdure which Periandro discovers amid darkness on emerging from Antonio's refuge on the smoldering island, to the apocalyptic tree of life and waters of life as well as to their sacramental descendant, the waters of bap-

[23] I treat this dimension of the scene in *Cervantes, Aristotle, and the "Persiles,"* Ch. VIII.

tism. Moreover, his prophecy concludes by looking forward to the pilgrims' successful achievement of their goal. Thus it takes its place in the series of triumphant visions, which begin with Periandro's gaze toward heaven as he is hoisted from the underground sepulcher and continue in Antonio's wife's statement of the Credo, in the pilgrims' worship before the altar of the hermits, in the joyous vision of Portugal, in the worship of the Sacrament following the salvation in the tower; and it announces the climactic vision of Rome from the hilltop, which will follow shortly.

The adventure of Soldino's cave is Cervantes' final monument to the synthesis of the classical and Christian traditions which Christian humanism had achieved and which enjoyed its final and fullest flowering in the age of the Counterreformation. In this world-weary soldier who has faithfully served Charles V for many years, we observe the harmonious coexistence of classical antiquity's ideal of moral perfection on earth and the Christian awareness that earthly existence is but a prelude to the life that is to follow. Dedication to one's duty within the state and within history, obedience to one's king, belief in furthering God's purposes through both active and contemplative pursuits, all characterize the aged seer. The rich interweave of the Christian and the classical is visible in his prophecy; for not only does it announce the successful completion of the pilgrims' journey, but also, in its clear overtones of Anchises' prophecy, associates once again the myth of Aeneas, the secular hero, with their quest. It is well to recall the Policarpo episode, in which both the biblical and the Virgilian quests were in the background of the events of the narration, as well as the numerous evocations of the *Aeneid* in Periandro's recitation.

The pilgrims' triumphant vision of Rome, accompanied by the sonnet restating the traditional association of the Eternal City with the City of God, is the climactic moment of the romance. Nevertheless, some of the most difficult ordeals yet await the heroes in the heart of the city. The biblical note of bondage sounds once again as Periandro is threatened by the temptations of the "new Egyptian," Hipólita, and her false paradise.[24] Like his

[24] In this scene Cervantes creates an entirely artificial paradise as the place of bondage. Hipólita's servant Zabulón, who as Jew and husband of a witch is associated with the demonic forces opposing the protagonists, leads the victim into a storeroom, where he discovers art treasures created by such masters as Polignotus, Apeles, Rafael, and Michelangelo. The narrator immediately voices the Renaissance commonplace that art guarantees the eternity of fame and hence is the conqueror of time. At this moment the garden paradise motifs appear. An astonished Periandro notes an agreeable harmony in the song of a variety of birds in richly adorned cages and recalls the gardens of the Hesperides and the sorceress Falerina. Thus through allusion the tradition of the garden paradise as temptation is evoked, and the protagonist undergoes an experience which in its moral implications is similar to those of such contemporary figures as Tasso's Rinaldo in Armida's garden and Spenser's Guyon in the Bower of Bliss (see A. Bartlett Giamatti, op. cit., Chs. IV, V). What is particularly interesting here is the association of the noblest forms of art and the Renaissance faith in art as a conqueror of time with the false values of the paradise and its demonic forces. Cervantes momentarily approaches an ascetic tonality which is uncharacteristic of both the *Persiles* as a whole and his other writings. As a false paradise Hipólita's storeroom recreates the island paradise of Periandro's dream and represents a demonic counterweight to the various true paradises of the work, namely, the Island of the Hermits, the cave of Soldino, and the Celestial Paradise as described in Feliciana's song.

biblical ancestor, Joseph, Periandro flees the ardent advances of the temptress, leaving behind his cloak. The
scorned courtesan promptly accuses him of theft, and he
is menaced with imprisonment. Following Periandro's
ordeal, Auristela must undergo a "near-death," enduring
a dreadful illness, which a Jewish sorceress inflicts upon
her and which disfigures her beyond recognition.

The pilgrims' final struggle occurs in the scene of tu-
mult before the Basilica of Saint Paul.[25] In this monu-

[25] As the impressive studies of Castro and Bataillon have shown,
Cervantes' Christianity is not of the militant type celebrated in the
Spanish drama of his contemporaries. In Part Two of the *Quixote*
it is not the patron saint of Spain, Santiago, the Moorslayer, who
draws Don Quixote's highest praise but rather St. Paul, "caballero
andante por la vida, y santo a pie quedo por la muerte, trabajador
incansable en la viña del Señor, doctor de las gentes, a quien sir-
vieron de escuelas los cielos y de catedrático y maestro que le en-
señase, el mismo Jesucristo" (II, 954). The emphasis on St. Paul at
the conclusion of the *Persiles* and the conciliatory attitude toward
Protestantism visible throughout the work are, to my mind, important indications that the impact of Erasmus on Cervantes'
religious development survives in his final and most orthodox work
(for the influence of Erasmus and St. Paul on Cervantes' religious
ideas, see Marcel Bataillon, *Erasmo y España* [México, 1966], pp.
777-801; Américo Castro, *El pensamiento de Cervantes* [Madrid,
1925], Ch. VI, and *Cervantes y los casticismos españoles*, pp.
101-106). To be sure, Protestantism is presented as a misfortune;
the Christians of northern Europe are in need of enlightenment.
However, reconciliation would appear to be a goal worth striving
for. After all, Persiles and Sigismunda's pilgrimage is in part
motivated by a desire to set aright the Christianity of the northern
world. At the same time, although the pilgrimage leads to Rome,
its real end is the Basilica of St. Paul rather than St. Peter's Cathe-
dral. In the introduction to his German translation of the *Persiles*,
Anton Rothbauer suggests the interesting possibility that Cervantes

mental setting Periandro receives what appears to be a mortal wound from Hipólita's jealous lover Pirro, and the Prince Magsimino, whose warlike figure has loomed menacingly in the background of the heroes' pilgrimage, finally overtakes Auristela, his betrothed. At this moment of potential disaster, instead of seeking to avenge the flight of his brother and his betrothed, Prince Magsimino announces that he is dying of a fever endemic to southern Italy and magnanimously joins the hands of his bleeding younger brother and Auristela, blessing their marriage. Periandro's wounds again prove to be curable ("... la fea muerte salió al encuentro al gallardo Persiles [Periandro] y le

---

wished to associate the pilgrimage of his "half-gentiles" with the travels of St. Paul in the New Testament. The "gentile saint's" description of his ordeals could well be applied to those of Cervantes' heroes: "Are they servants of Christ? I am a better one—I am talking like a madman—with far greater labors, far more imprisonments, with countless beatings, and often near death. Five times I have received at the hands of the Jews the forty lashes less one. Three times I have been beaten with rods; once I was stoned. Three times I have been shipwrecked; a night and a day I have been adrift at sea; on frequent journeys, in danger from rivers, danger from robbers, danger from my own people, danger from Gentiles, danger in the city, danger in the wilderness, danger at sea, danger from false brethren; in toil and hardship, through many a sleepless night, in hunger and thirst, often without food, in cold and exposure" (2 Cor. 11). In the Church of St. Paul this passage is read during one of the Easter Masses for catechumens. Allusions to Easter are frequent in the southern adventures, and Periandro and Auristela could be described as catechumens in their desire for Catholic instruction. Rothbauer goes on to suggest that there is a strong ecumenical message in the *Persiles*. The northern Europeans must be reconciled with the Catholic Church through instruction and not through war (see Cervantes, *Die Mühen und Leiden des Persiles und der Sigismunda* [Stuttgart, 1963], pp. 58-83).

derribó en tierra, y enterró a Magsimino" [p. 474]), and the marriage is celebrated.

Thus in Rome the cycle of disaster and restoration that marks the seemingly endless series of "trabajos" in the lives of the heroes comes to a halt. Moreover, its final upward turn brings with it the completion of the larger cycle which embraces the entire action and which has been repeated in each individual adventure. For the triumphant marriage of the heroes delivers the northern kingdoms from their sufferings. The wars which have menaced the kingdoms for over two years have ended. The marriage of Persiles and Sigismunda [at the conclusion of their quest, Periandro and Auristela assume their real names], which unifies the kingdoms and produces children, grandchildren, and great-grandchildren,[26] removes the threat of sterility which the isolation of an all-male royal family in Tile and an all-female royal family in Frislanda has presented. Moreover, the oppressive ruler, Prince Magsimino, who in the cycle of the total action has a role analogous to that of the various demonic agents in the individual adventures,[27] has been overcome and

[26] The romance ends with the following words: ". . . [Sigismunda] vivió en compañía de su esposo Persiles hasta que biznietos le alargaron los días, pues los vio en su larga y feliz posteridad" (p. 475).

[27] "Magsimino, a quien la aspereza de sus costumbres en algún modo le [Auristela] hacían aborrecible" (p. 467). Magsimino is constantly occupied in waging war. His ailment at the conclusion is symbolic of his sinister role. It is interesting that the dying Magsimino addresses his brother and intended bride as "Verdaderos hijos y hermanos míos," as he proclaims their marriage, accession to the throne, and the unification of the kingdoms. In Magsimino's sudden appearance in the role of the ailing father giving way to

105

replaced by the enlightened heroes. And finally, the dark kingdoms themselves, which are analogous to the numerous places of bondage in the individual adventures, are illuminated by the Catholic enlightenment with which Auristela has been entrusted following her initiation into the mysteries of the penitentiaries, and become analogous to the many holy places in the adventures.

On the allegorical level, which has been constantly maintained in the background of the action by Christian and classical myths and archetypal imagery and symbols, the heroes' entrance into Rome represents the fulfillment of the Christian view of human history, the ultimate triumph of God and the New Jerusalem over Satan and the city of Babylon, and the ascent of the individual human soul to the state of Blessedness. Rome, the simulacrum of the Celestial City, is the point at which all unfulfilled desire ends, the center at which the soul in its endless movements during its separation from God can at last find repose. At the ethical level of the allegory of the *Persiles*, the entrance into Rome represents a vindication of the values of patience, faith in God, and devotion to one's duty, which must guide suffering humanity through the darkness of the world of temporality.

The three levels of the allegorical meaning of the *Persiles* (in traditional terms, the allegorical, the tropological, and the anagogical [see above, pp. 31-34]) are neatly summarized in the mysteries revealed to Auristela in Rome. While they provide the enlightenment which the

---

Periandro, Cervantes is repeating in the *Persiles* an archetypal theme of romance—the aged king who must be replaced by a youthful redeemer who can restore peace and fertility to his blighted kingdom.

heroine has been seeking throughout her wanderings (it should be recalled that Feliciana's song, a poetic expression of the same mysteries, remained incomprehensible to her), they moreover reveal to the reader the meaning of the *Persiles*, offering him a key to its exegesis. The penitentiaries explain to Auristela the history of the universe, from Lucifer's rebellion through the Crucifixion to the Last Judgment; they advise her that "en sólo conocer y ver a Dios está la suma gloria, y todos los medios que para este fin se encaminan son los buenos . . . como son los de la caridad, de la honestidad, y el de la virginidad"; and they describe the destiny of the individual soul: "Nuestras almas . . . como aquí me han enseñado, siempre están en continuo movimiento, y no pueden parar sino en Dios, como en su centro. En esta vida, los deseos son infinitos, y unos se encadenan de otros y se eslabonan, y van formando una cadena que tal vez llega al cielo, y tal se sume en el infierno" (pp. 458-459).

CHAPTER THREE

Episodes

THE NORTH

IN MY analysis of the structure of the *Persiles* in relation to Cervantes' Aristotelian theories of unity, I concluded that most of the episodes are not "nacidos de los mesmos sucesos" and that in their independence and length they divert the reader's attention from the development of the main plot, destroying the effect of suspense which Heliodorus' *Aethiopica* had achieved and which all contemporary theorists set as the goal of dispositional techniques. I also maintained that aesthetic coherence in the maze of narrative threads forming the surface of the *Persiles* must be sought in relation to non-Aristotelian[1] criteria of unity, and suggested analogy and recurrence as principles of structural unity and the motif of "los trabajos" as a principle of thematic unity.

Nearly all the episodes of the *Persiles* repeat the cyclical rhythm which has been traced through the main plot. In reenacting the cycle of disaster and restoration against the background of the Christian myth of fall and redemption, the episodes form a series of units, each an analogy of the total movement of the *Persiles* (restoration of order in the northern kingdoms and redemption of man) and an analogy of the individual adventures of the protagonists ("near-death" and salvation). The statement of dual motifs corresponding to the two moments of the

[1] I am referring of course to the Renaissance interpretation of the *Poetics* when I use the term "Aristotelian."

cycle, a process which I have likened to the statement of subject and answer in fugal composition, is repeated in the episodes. Death-resurrection, bondage-liberation, darkness-light, despair-joy, sea-land, wilderness-city, sterility-fertility are the familiar motifs sounded in the seemingly endless series of episodes. As in the main plot, the first member of the duality is dominant in the first half, or the northern adventures, and the second member begins to dominate in the southern adventures. Examination of a few episodes will make this process clear.

The four independent episodes of the northern adventures are those of the Spaniard Antonio, the Italian dancing master Rutilio, the French knight Renato, and the Hibernian maiden Transila. All are borne through moments of "near-death" on quests to the northern regions of the world, where the trajectories of their lives and those of the protagonists intersect. The quests of Antonio and Rutilio have a pronounced expiatory character. In a moment of uncontrollable anger the Spaniard wounds a noble who has addressed him as "vos." In flight aboard a vessel sailing for England, he provokes and strikes a member of the crew for no apparent reason, and the captain of the ship sets him adrift in a lifeboat. Antonio describes the days and nights during which he is at the mercy of the sea as a lingering death: ". . . era una muerte dilatada mi vida" (p. 76). Loneliness, the violence and the immensity of the sea, and darkness fill him with terror, and he implores heaven for deliverance which does not come (". . . vino la noche escura, halléme solo en la mitad de la inmensidad de aquellas aguas . . . Alcé los ojos al cielo" [p. 75]). He is tormented by a nightmare, in which he suffers "mil géneros de muertes espantosas, pero todas en el agua" and is torn to pieces by wolves. A violent storm raises the "furious water" of the sea about him and drives his boat toward a rugged island overrun by ferocious wolves.

At the moment of disaster, amid the familiar subject motifs of darkness, the sea, despair, bondage, storm, the sterile landscape, and the menacing monster, the voice of the answer begins to sound. The night is less obscure, the sea becomes calm, the wind abates, and Antonio discovers the stars shining in the heavens. In this "dudosa luz de la noche" the wanderer makes out the forms of wolves hovering above him on the very cliff which offers a haven for his boat. A voice emerges from one of the wolves advising him to seek refuge elsewhere and to thank God for saving him from the teeth and claws of the beasts.

With the wolf's pronouncement the most harrowing part of Antonio's expiatory "near-death" concludes. In his wrath he has descended to the level of the beast and confronted his sin in its most hideous form. Now through repentance and God's mercy he can begin his ascent upward toward the redeemed condition of humanity. The ascent will be difficult, for it will demand years of bondage and expiation on the island of the barbarians, which Antonio describes as the abyss into which he has been flung by Fortune's wheel (p. 73). Ricla, the maiden who, like an "ángel del cielo," "bella como el sol," "mansa como una cordera," saves the Spaniard from death as his boat finally drifts ashore, bringing him bread ("hecho a su modo, que no era de trigo") and leading him to the circular garden and brook, informs Periandro that she and Antonio have been awaiting the happy day when a deliverer will come to free them from their "prisión."

At this point the episode of Antonio intersects with the main plot, for just as Antonio delivers the heroes from their "near-death" in the slaughter and fire of the barbarians, Periandro and Auristela have arrived to deliver him from his island bondage. From this moment on, Antonio, Ricla, and their children share the "trabajos" of the heroes until the group arrives in Ocaña, where in a joyous scene of recognition Antonio is reunited with his father, mother, and sisters. Here the only son is restored to the family, which is threatened by that unfulfillment which Cervantes generally associates with a family in which there are no male heirs. Antonio's return from the wilderness is rewarded by heaven immediately, as one of the surviving brothers of the noble whom he had attacked sixteen years before marries his daughter, elevating her to his rank in society and reconciling the families. The narrator assures us that this reconciliation and restoration have been accomplished by providential design: ". . . la disposición del cielo, que, con causas a nosotros secretas, ordena y dispone las cosas de la tierra, ordenó y quiso que . . ." (p. 337).

Antonio's expiatory quest, which begins with the downward turn of Fortune's wheel and concludes by the workings of God's Providence, is both structurally and thematically analogous to the quest of the protagonists, within which it is contained. The cyclical movement from disorder to restoration of order, from the wilderness to civilization, from variance with the divine order to the celebration of the divine order, from sterility to fertility in

111

the movement toward Catholic marriage, is presented in a narrative structure that begins at a low moment in the cycle and moves both backward in time, illuminating the origins of the disorder, and forward toward the restoration.

Like that of Antonio, the quest of Rutilio begins with a fall into sin and bears him to the dark edges of the earth, where he must suffer a similar penance before being delivered from the island of the barbarians by the protagonists. Here the sin is not wrath, but lust, and his ordeals of expiation begin with imprisonment and a sentence of death. The retribution of society is merely the first phase of his sufferings. Following his nocturnal escape from jail, he falls into the clutches of a witch, who, with the aid of the devil, bears him on a four-hour flight from Italy to a dim landscape in Norway and attempts to seduce him. At this moment the witch assumes the hideous form of a wolf, and Rutilio desperately fights off her advances, succeeding in killing her after a bitter struggle. This point in Rutilio's quest corresponds to that in which Antonio drifts toward the island of the wolves and must spend a long night beholding the bestial condition to which he has fallen. The same motifs of loneliness, darkness ("la noche se alargava"—once again, the endless night of the Apocalypse), horror, and the diabolical monster accompany Rutilio's vigil.

Estuve esperando el día muchas horas, pero nunca acababa de llegar, ni por los horizontes se descubría señal de que el sol viniese. Apartéme de aquel cadáver, porque me causaba horror y espanto el tenerlo cerca de mí. Volvía muy a menudo los ojos al cielo, contemplaba el movimiento de las estrellas, y parecíame, según el curso que habían hecho, que ya había de ser de día. Estando en esta confusión. . . .   (p. 91)

The searching gaze toward heaven and the motif of the stars announce the beginning of Rutilio's ascent, which, like that of Antonio, is slow and arduous. He cannot yet return from the northern lands, where evil witches abound and where "esperar la claridad del sol, por entonces era esperanza vana" (p. 92),[2] but enters a city "donde toda la gente andaba por las calles con palos de tea encendidos en las manos" (p. 93), and passes into the employment of a goldsmith. Given the symbolic implications of Rutilio's quest and the traditional infernal connections of the smithy, Rutilio's place of employment is in

---

[2] Here and in the following passage describing the geography of the northern lands we observe a good example of a learned digression which serves the purposes of instruction and the verisimilar marvelous, demanded by the literary theories which Cervantes embraced, and at the same time functions in the symbolic movement of the romance. The symbolic use of the northern landscape was enabled by the current association of the geographically real lands of the north with darkness and obscurity (see A. Castro, "Noruega, símbolo de la oscuridad," *Revista de Filología Española*, 6 [1919], 184-185 and L. Spitzer, "La Norvège comme Symbole de L'Obscurité," *Revista de Filología Española*, 9 [1922], 316-317). For their association with demonic forces, see Antonio de Torquemada: ". . . en esta tierra parece que el demonio está más suelto y tiene mayor libertad que en otras partes, y así, quieren decir algunos que es la principal habitación de los demonios . . . de aquellos partes ha de venir el Anticristo." Rutilio's words "maléficas hechiceras, de las cuales hay mucha abundancia en estas septentrionales partes" (p. 92) echo Torquemada's "hay muchos hechiceros y nigrománticos en todas las tierras del Norte" (*Jardín de flores curiosas*, ed. A. de Amezúa [Madrid, 1943], p. 288).

113

reality one more of the various hells in which he must suffer. After two months Rutilio and his employer set out on a business trip, and their ship is buffeted by a storm which lasts forty days. Once again we observe in the background of the adventures the archetypal flood of purgation and the deliverance of the elect, which lay behind Periandro's escape from his executioners in the opening scene and the heroes' escape from the scuttled ship and the lascivious soldiers.

Only Rutilio survives the shipwreck, crawling ashore on the island of the barbarians to spend three years of penance before being delivered by Periandro. The corpse hanging from the tree, which Rutilio immediately discovers, announces the island as a realm of death ("me puso delante mil géneros de muertes," a vision which recalls Antonio's dream of "mil géneros de muertes espantosas, pero todas en el agua"). His donning the dress of animal skins which clothes the cadaver and his decision to feign deafness and muteness symbolize the descent to bestiality inherent in his sin. We need not recall the words of the dog Berganza describing speech as a divine gift, which human beings alone among God's creatures enjoy, to see in Rutilio's decision the conditions of a dreadful penance.

Following his release from the island of the barbarians, Rutilio, like Antonio, shares the "trabajos" of the heroes. When they reach the Island of the Hermits, he is deeply affected by Renato's life of contemplation and decides to remain on the island, worshiping God in peace and keeping the flame of the lighthouse burning for the salvation of victims of the sea. Spatially, Rutilio's quest from a demonic order to an apocalyptic order can be neatly plotted, its vertical axis running from the dark depths of the dungeon and the forge of the smithy to the blazing pinnacle of the lighthouse and the altar and images of the mountain chapel, its horizontal axis running from the hanging tree on the barren island of the barbarians to the fruit-bearing trees of Renato's paradise.

The way in which apocalyptic symbols generate their demonic counterweights in the *Persiles* is observable in yet another facet of Rutilio's adventures. He is a dancing master and himself affirms the lofty function of the dance in the social world: ". . . que la gentileza, gallardía y disposición del cuerpo, en los bailes más que en otros pasos se señalan." Following his fall Rutilio must spend three years entertaining the barbarians with somersaults ("cabriolas"), certainly the demonic equivalent of the dance.[3] In the total context of the *Persiles* the somersault is a counterweight to the dances in Toledo, an image of universal harmony (see above, p. 90).

Cervantes does not care to give the quest of Rutilio the triumphant conclusion which we observe in Antonio's return to Ocaña, and the Italian disappears from the surface of the narrative. However, it is significant that in the final scene of the romance he does appear in Rome. Thus the cycle of descent to darkness and ascent to light, of entry into the wilderness and return to civilization, on which the main plot is based, is completed. As in the episode of Antonio, the structure of the episode of Rutilio is analogous to that of the quest of the heroes, which con-

---

[3] In the *Gitanilla* the demonic character of the Gypsy world is repeatedly brought out by Cervantes. In order to enter that world the hero must undergo an initiation, which includes garroting and two somersaults (see *Obras completas*, p. 789). Sancho Panza reminds us that the world's first acrobat was Lucifer (II, 698).

tains it, as from a low point the narration moves backward toward the fall and forward toward the restoration.

In the episode of the French courtier Renato, the expiatory nature of the quest from civilization to the wilderness and back is less pronounced, and hence the analogies between it and that of the heroes are stronger. Unlike Antonio and Rutilio the French knight commits no sin, and his sufferings would appear to have no logic other than that of offering proof of the ultimate inscrutability of a divine providence which can never be questioned ("¡Oh soberanos cielos! ¡Oh juicios de Dios inescrutables!" [p. 262]) and of providing him with a test of faith which he must survive in order to reach a higher level of consciousness and participation in divinity.[4]

Placing absolute faith in God, he defends the honor of his beloved against a calumniator and is defeated. In disbelief that God can vindicate falsehood and dishonor, lonely and confused, Renato lies defeated on a distant field in Germany, longing for death and refusing to raise his eyes to heaven. At this moment of "near-death" and despair, the familiar motif of darkness reappears, recalling the darkness of Periandro's prison, the prolonged night shrouding Antonio's shelter, the nights on the islands of snow, and the endless night of Rutilio: ". . . el claro cielo, para mí estaba cubierto de obscuras tinieblas" (p. 263). He

---

[4] "Con esto dio fin a su plática Renato, y con esto dio ocasión a que todos los circunstantes se admirasen de su suceso, no porque les pareciese nuevo dar castigos el cielo contra la esperanza de los pensamientos humanos, pues se sabe que por una de dos causas vienen los que parecen males a las gentes: a los malos, por castigo, y a los buenos, por mejora" (p. 264).

sets out toward the north seeking to end his life and "to bury his name" and arrives at the Island of the Hermits, where his spiritual rebirth occurs amid the trees, flowers, and springs of the paradisiacal region. A year later his beloved Eusebia renounces the world of the court and joins Renato on the island, where they spend ten years in an ascetic marriage, worshiping God and awaiting the eternal life: "Dormimos aparte, comemos juntos, hablamos del cielo, menospreciamos la tierra, y confiados en la misericordia de Dios, esperamos la vida eterna" (p. 264).

The tone of *contemptus mundi*, which sounds in these words, is entirely uncharacteristic of the *Persiles*, in which the movement is toward an affirmation of a worldly order and worldly values sanctioned by God and symbolized by the city, to which nearly all the wanderers return. Hence it comes as no surprise that Renato introduces his narration as a tale of suffering told in the midst of suffering ("no los [trabajos] cuento fuera de la borrasca, sino en mitad de la tormenta" [p. 261]), that he proceeds to refer to his present "siniestro estado" as one of misfortune as he welcomes his brother, and that the latter announces the death and repentance of Renato's adversary as the end of his "pena." The restoration of Renato's honor by the king of France is celebrated by all the wanderers and inspires in Arnaldo a rhetorical outburst on the value of worldly honor: "... la honra perdida y vuelta a cobrar con estremo, no tiene bien alguno la tierra que se le iguale" (p. 271). The hermits decide to abandon the island immediately and to return to the court of France, where the king is waiting to receive them. The "trabajos" of Renato and his quest from civilization to the wilderness and back are presented as a vindication of the "secretos juicios de Dios" in much the same way as are those of the protagonists.[5]

As in the episodes of Antonio and Rutilio, the point at which the trajectory of Renato and that of the main characters intersect is a point of correspondence in their respective quests. Renato's island paradise is a moment of restoration in the cyclical movement of the "trabajos" of the protagonists, who find here a haven after the flight from the burning palace of Policarpo and a prefiguration of the goal of their quest. During this moment Renato's spiritual resurrection has been completed, he is freed from bondage, and he can join the pilgrims in the moment of triumph as they set out to return to civilization. Similarly the structural pattern of the episode itself follows that of the main plot and the other episodes, as the narrative begins at a moment of bondage and moves backward toward the fall and forward toward the restoration.

Transila's quest is similar to those of the protagonists and Renato in that her sufferings result from no sin and are sent by heaven to reveal the cyclical, incomplete condition of human life in temporality: (". . . las buenas andanzas no vienen sin el contrapeso de desdichas, las cuales tienen jurisdición y un modo de licencia de entrarse por los buenos sucesos, para darnos a entender que, ni el bien es eterno ni el mal durable" [p. 116]). However, its thematic focus is less essential, for it is concerned not only with the individual and the providential order, but also with the relationship between a social institution and that order. On the one hand, Transila's quest is a celebration of

[5] In describing Auristela's near-fatal illness in Rome, the narrator informs us that in reality it is not the Jewish sorceress who has inflicted her with it, but the will of God (p. 457).

Divine Providence, the sacrament of marriage, and the virtues of chastity and perseverance; on the other, it is a critical examination of marriage as a social institution.

Transila's bridal chamber becomes a place of bondage as the relatives of her husband, in accordance with the law of her island kingdom, enter to gather the fruits of her virginity. The maiden flees into a small boat, "which heaven provided," and an obliging current sweeps her away from both her betrothed and her tormentors. Like Antonio she spends the night at the mercy of the sea. When she drifts ashore, she discovers that her ordeals have only begun, as the inhabitants sell her to pirates who in turn sell her to the barbarians of the island where the protagonists meet her.

Transila's role as an advocate of Christian marriage and as a heroic virgin, separated from her beloved and harassed by various lustful antagonists, is very similar to that of Auristela in the main plot. However, her affinities with Preciosa of the *Gitanilla* are even more pronounced. In both the novella and this episode, Cervantes celebrates Christian marriage as a foundation of social order, one which is sanctioned both by reason and grace.[6] The law of

---

[6] In the Transila episode Cervantes does not deal directly with the sacramental foundation of marriage, although it is certainly present by implication. At another point in the work, when marriage is introduced as a theme, he does indeed emphasize its importance. In words very similar to those of Preciosa, Periandro offers advice to the irrascible Pole Ortel Banedre: "Pero esto debe de ser en otras religiones que en la cristiana, entre las cuales los matrimonios son una manera de concierto y conveniencia, como lo es el de alquilar una casa o otra alguna heredad; pero en la religión católica, el casamiento es sacramento que sólo se desata con la muerte" (p. 325).

the barbarians, which permits the abuse of the bride by the relatives of the groom, and the law of the Gypsies, which founds marriage in carnal desire and allows its bond to be broken when the appetite is sated, are not only corruptions of the sacrament, the "santo yugo," which, as Preciosa points out, is a means of preserving chastity even as it is surrendered and a bond which endures for a lifetime, but also violations of reason and natural law, the foundations of social order. In resignation Transila's father Mauricio rationalizes his acceptance of the barbarous custom of his society in words suggesting its opposition to natural law: "la costumbre es otra naturaleza." Transila rebukes her tormentors, whose "deshonestas y bárbaras costumbres van contra las que guarda cualquier bien ordenada república," and asserts: "la razón, puesta en la punta desta lanza, defenderá mi partido" (pp. 113-114). Preciosa rejects the Gypsy marriage in similar terms: ". . . no me rijo por la bárbara e insolente licencia que estos mis parientes se han tomado de dejar las mujeres, o castigarlas, cuando se les antoja," and her comrade Clemente defends Catholic marriage as sanctioned by "la bien intencionada naturaleza." The connection between Preciosa's view of marriage and wedded love and the well-being of the state is most forcefully presented in the maiden's song celebrating the birth of Philip IV.[7]

Following Transila's defense of chastity and marriage, Rosamunda rises to defend the law which the maiden fled. Finding in the sexual act nothing more than a source of physical pleasure and comparing the instruction of a woman to the training of a horse, her speech is analogous to that of the Gypsy elder, who, in opposition to Preciosa,

[7] See *Obras completas*, pp. 776-777, 790, 798.

sees marriage as a means to sexual gratification and asserts that the Gypsies murder unfaithful wives and bury them as if they were wild animals. As an example of what uncontrolled lust leads to, Rosamunda is a vindication of Transila's belief that restraint and Christian marriage are the cornerstones of the well-ordered state; for the English courtesan "mandó al rey y por añadidura a todo el reino; puso leyes, quitó leyes, levantó caídos viciosos y derribó levantados virtuosos" (p. 118).

The presence in the *Persiles* of the historical figure Rosemond Clifford, mistress of Henry II of England, is surprising, as Antonio's narration has just placed its events in the middle of the sixteenth century. Whether Cervantes' concern for allegorical meaning overrode his preoccupation with plausibility in this case or whether he assumed his audience did not know medieval history well enough to discover the chronological inconsistency is difficult to determine. (Contemporary theorists did in fact recommend that the poet employ medieval history as the basis for his plot because the audience's knowledge of it was very limited.)[8] It is certain, however, that the allegorical function of this character is most pronounced and that, aside from Periandro's dream, she is one of the few cases in which the *Persiles* approaches pure allegory.[9] She appears in an emblematic pose, enchained to an exiled satiric poet (satire thrives on lust and debases poetry; both should be banished from the well-ordered republic), and her brief participation in the *Persiles* is reduced to the symbolic act of attempting to seduce an innocent youth. She is van-

[8] See Tasso, *Del poema eroico*, pp. 98-99; Francisco Cascales, *Tablas poéticas*, p. 134.

[9] See Carlos Romero, op. cit., p. lxxiii.

quished by heroic chastity and dies, joining the various demonic antagonists whose cadavers litter the paths of the heroes of the work.

Within the total context of the *Persiles*, the barbarous law which victimizes Transila, and which Rosamunda defends, is related to the prophecy by which the barbarians organize their society, and both are demonic counterweights to the divine wisdom which Auristela receives from the penitentiaries in Rome, as well as to the Christian sacraments—the Eucharist and marriage. Following Transila's reunion with her father and her betrothed in Golandia, she accompanies the pilgrims on to Policarpo's kingdom, shares in their ordeals there, and departs for her country as the others journey toward Portugal. Toward the end of the work we learn that she and her husband have decided to leave the barbarous kingdom and live in the Christian society of England.[10] Once again we observe the recurrent structural pattern: the narration of Transila's quest begins at a low point in her fortunes and moves backward toward the cause of her sufferings and forward toward her reunion with her husband.

[10] The fact that in Transila's quest England is presented as a counterweight to the kingdom which upholds the *ius primae noctis* is one more indication of Cervantes' conciliatory attitude toward the Christians of northern Europe. At no point are they given the demonic characteristics usually attributed to barbarians, Turks, and Jews in the *Persiles*. To be recalled are Cervantes' favorable treatment of Queen Elizabeth I of England in *La española inglesa* and Ricote's praise of the religious tolerance which he discovered in Germany: ". . . llegué a Alemania, y allí me pareció que se podía vivir con más libertad, porque sus habitadores no miran en muchas delicadezas: cada uno vive como quiere, porque en la mayor parte della se vive con libertad de conciencia" (II, 933).

THE SOUTH

The remaining episodes of the *Persiles* continue to re-enact the movement which we have observed in the main plot, in its individual adventures, and in the subordinate plots of the northern episodes. In keeping with the overall ascending movement in the main plot, the dominant moment of the recurrent cycle in the southern episodes is that of restoration. It is well to recall that the triumphant conclusions of the quests of Antonio, Rutilio, Renato, and Transila actually occur in the second part of the work. Indeed what has been said about the shift in tonality in the main plot—from minor (or tragic) in the first part to major (or comic) in the second part—is applicable to the episodes. If in the northern episodes the dominant notes are darkness, exile, penance, demonic forces, fear, sterility, separation of lovers, and the wilderness, in the southern episodes we discern a modulation toward a major tonality, as the notes of light, vision of divinity, reconciliation, atonement, joy, fertility, and marriage begin to sound triumphantly.

The first episode, that of Feliciana de la Voz, establishes the new tone; for it culminates in marriage, birth, and a vision of the apocalyptic City of God. In the first chapter I observed how the narrative thread of this episode is interwoven with that of the main plot, presenting it as an example of Cervantes' technique of fragmentary narration. It remains for me here to point out how the adventure repeats once more the cyclical statement and answer of theme observable at nearly every moment in the *Persiles*.

Once again the cycle begins at a low point. The familiar motif of darkness introduces it: ". . . se cerró la noche con

123

tanta escuridad que los detuvo . . . Las tinieblas de la noche, y un ruido que sintieron, les detuvo el paso" (p. 287). From the darkness, a man appears, deposits a crying baby with the pilgrims, and vanishes. Shortly thereafter a disheveled young woman emerges from the surrounding forest and asks the group for shelter. The pilgrims and their shepherd hosts hide the fugitive in the hollow trunk of an oak tree and cover her with the skins of sheep. Feliciana passes a night of fear in the hollow, as her pursuers arrive and, failing to find her, ride on in their search.

Although her fear is so great that, on the following morning, the maiden "apenas osaba ver del sol la claridad hermosa" (p. 292), she emerges and relates her story, revealing that her father has attempted to marry her against her will and that she has just given birth to the child of the man whom she loves. Menaced by her father's knife and thoughts of suicide, she has fled into the night and desperately made her way toward a distant light, the fire of the shepherds.

In the "near-death" of Feliciana during the dark night of flight and imprisonment in the hollow of the tree, we observe the reenactment of Periandro's nights in the dungeon of the barbarians and the hut of Antonio, Antonio's helpless abandonment to the sea and darkness in the small boat, Rutilio's endless vigil on the dark plain of Norway, and Renato's discovery of darkness in God's heavens. The plight of the young woman is effectively associated with the motif of "trabajos," and the analogy is drawn between it and the main plot by Auristela's comment: "Paréceme . . . que los trabajos y los peligros no solamente tienen jurisdición en el mar, sino en toda la tierra" (p. 296), and her discourse on the wheel of Fortune, who "ciega y antojadiza" has cast the young girl from home, family, and lover down into the hollow of a tree, where she is menaced by "mosquitos del aire, y aun las lombrices de la tierra" (p. 296). The allusion to Fortune's wheel recalls the fall of Antonio and looks forward to the final scene of the *Persiles*, in which the narrator announces the unexpected denouement by stating the orthodox belief, of which the entire *Persiles* is a vindication: ". . . estas mudanzas tan estrañas, caen debajo del poder de aquella que comúnmente es llamada fortuna, que no es otra cosa sino un firme disponer del cielo" (p. 474).

As in all other cases, the cycle of "los trabajos" takes its turn. The night passes, the sun illuminates the landscape, and the restoration begins. The baby is saved, the pursuers vanish, and Feliciana joins the group of pilgrims. She still must suffer another moment of "near-death" as she kneels before the altar of Guadalupe to sing a hymn to the Virgin. Her persecutors recognize her voice, and her brother rushes toward her, knife in hand. In a tumultuous scene, in which the villagers, the police, the avenging father and brother, and the father of Feliciana's child converge on the helpless woman, a reconciliation is achieved, in which anger gives way to mercy, and fear for the loss of honor yields to the joy surrounding the birth of a child.

The conclusion of the Feliciana episode offers one of the purest illustrations of what Hatzfeld has called Cervantes' dynamic "*veni-vidi-vici*" style.[11] In the *Persiles* the style

[11] ". . . wo die gehäuften Kurzsätze einen hastig gedrängten Bericht geben, dem in Anbetracht der Fülle seines Inhalts tatsächlich die dynamische Kraft innewohnt (genau wie bei dem berühmten Cäsarwort), die dem Gedanken fast zu enge Form zu sprengen" (*"Don Quijote" als Wortkunstwerk*, p. 205). Another

often appears at climactic moments, punctuating with the
energy of its series of short parallel units, each containing
a verb in the preterite tense, the movement from "near-
death" to restoration. In this case, the moment of confusion
and doubt is reflected and prolonged in the syntactic disorder and the accumulation of gerunds, which underscore
the doubtful outcome of the action described:

> *Estando* en esta confusión, el padre *dando* voces por
> su hija, y su hermano por su hermana, y la justicia
> *defendiéndola* hasta saber el caso, por una parte de la
> plaza entraron hasta seis de a caballo, que los dos
> dellos fueron luego conocidos de todos, por ser el
> uno Don Francisco Pizarro y el otro Don Juan de
> Orellana, los cuales, *llegándose* al tumulto. . . .
> (p. 307)[12]

To return to the analogy which I have occasionally drawn
between the structure of the *Persiles* and the fugue, I
would liken this moment and style to the climactic stretto,
in which the excitement reaches highest intensity and
resolution seems to hang suspended before the triumphant
emergence of the coda. In the moment of restoration the
syntactic disorder and the gerunds give way to the concise,
paratactically constructed sentences and the series of preterites marking the conclusion of the action. To continue

---

good example can be found in the description of the delivery of the
pilgrims from the "ship-leviathan": ". . . limpiáronse los rostros,
fregáronse los ojos, estiraron los brazos, y como quien despierta de
un pesado sueño, miraron a todas partes, y hallóse Auristela en
los brazos de Arnaldo, Transila en los de Clodio . . ." (p. 164).

[12] The italics are mine, both here and in the passage quoted
below.

the analogy I would liken these preterites to the blocks of harmony of the coda.

Arrodillóse también ante su padre Feliciana, *derramó* lágrimas, *envió* suspiros, *vinieron* desmayos. La alegría *discurrió* por todos los circunstantes; *ganó* fama de prudente el padre, de prudente el hijo, y los amigos de discretos y bien hablados: *llevólos* el Corregidor a su casa, *regalólos* el prior del santo monasterio abundantísimamente; *visitaron* las reliquias los peregrinos, que son muchas, santísimas y ricas; *confesaron* sus culpas, *recibieron* los sacramentos, y en este tiempo, que fue el de tres días, *envió* Don Francisco por el niño. . . .   (pp. 308-309)

The most important moment in Feliciana's quest in relation to the symbolic movement of the *Persiles* is the hymn which she sings before the altar of the Virgin of Guadalupe. It is significant that Cervantes does not insert the song at the moment of its occurrence in the action but rather at the end of the episode. Again we observe the importance of theme and motif as principles of unity and plot development as opposed to chronology. The narrator states that the maiden sings some beautiful verses while the pilgrims adore the image of Christ but adds immediately: "los cuales dio después por escrito." As a hymn of liberation its proper position in the episode is at the moment of restoration; and so Cervantes has Auristela read it following the reconciliation of the maiden with her family and her return to society.

Representing one of the series of visionary moments through which the *Persiles* moves, Feliciana's song of the Celestial City and Paradise is linked imaginatively backward to the island paradise of Renato and the city of Lisbon and forward to the city of Rome. Moreover it is linked backward and forward to its demonic counter-weights—the island paradise of Periandro's dream and the artificial paradise of Hipólita. Introducing the divine order into the context of the *Persiles*, the hymn to the Virgin calls our attention to several minor details of the melodramatic episode which suggest that Cervantes had Christ in mind at this point in the composition of the work: the infant menaced by the knife of the enraged father (Herod), the flight of the parents toward Portugal, the shelter given them by the shepherds, the concealment of the child by the shepherds, the triumphant reappearance of the missing child "on the third day," the allusion to baptism, and the approach of Easter.

The same cyclical pattern of fall and ascent can be observed in the episodes of Ortel Banedre and Augustina Ambrosia. The familiar motifs of darkness and a hostile, enclosing space accompany their "near-deaths." That of the maiden occurs in the cart which bears her and some other prisoners to the executioner and the galleys. Huddled in the corner, Augustina smears her face with axle grease[13] and refuses to eat, claiming that she is awaiting death and that she wants to be as ugly as possible in death. Similarly Ortel Banedre, the irascible Pole, must spend a dark night of suffering following the turn of Fortune's wheel which directs the fatal thrust of his sword (". . . la

---

[13] The axle grease could be termed a very "mimetic variation" of a recurrent motif. It recalls the dust which covers Periandro's face as he lies in the dungeon of the barbarians and the first gesture of the victims who are delivered from the "ship-leviathan"—"limpiáronse los rostros."

ciega noche y la fortuna más ciega a la luz de mi mejor suerte, sin saber yo adónde, encaminó la punta de mi espada a la vista de mi contrario" [p. 316]). In fear and confusion, lost in the dark passages of an unknown city, he makes his way toward a light, where he finds shelter. Ortel Banedre's flight through menacing space toward a distant light recreates the heroes' flight on the island of the barbarians to the illuminated refuge of Antonio, their flight from the blazing kingdom of Policarpo toward the lighthouse of the Island of the Hermits, Feliciana's flight through the forest toward the fires of the shepherds' camp, Antonio's lonely voyage beneath the dim stars of the northern skies, and Periandro's gaze toward the light of heaven following his ascent from the dungeon. Here the enclosing space, characteristic of the center of the labyrinths through which the many characters of the *Persiles* must make their way—the tree trunk, the cave, the small boat, the ship-leviathan, the small cart, and the prison—is recreated in a hollow recess in the wall of a room covered by a tapestry (". . . alcé el tapiz, hallé el hueco, estrechéme en él, recogí el aliento, y comencé a encomendarme a Dios" [p. 317]).

The pursuers arrive to announce to Ortel's benefactor that the victim of the fugitive is her son. Like his choleric counterpart of the northern episodes, Antonio adrift at sea, Ortel has the vision of "mil géneros de muertes" which menace him. However, like Antonio in the night of suffering, he confronts his sin, prays to God and receives divine mercy. The dead man is described by his mother as a man of anger and arrogance and represents to Ortel what the wolves represent to Antonio, the bestial condition to which he himself has fallen. The words of the mother renouncing vengeance and recommending that the fugitive depart from his present "encerramiento" recall the words of the miraculous voice that emerges from the wolf to announce Antonio's ascent. Like Antonio, Ortel embarks on an expiatory quest, serving many years in the Portuguese army in the New World.[14]

[14] The history of Ortel Banedre is based on a novella by Giraldi Cintio (*Gli Ecatommiti*, [Firenze, 1834] VI, vi, 301-304). It is instructive to compare the versions; for the differences between them reveal how Cervantes creatively assimilated literary sources to his major theme and structure. Giraldi's novella focuses on the mother, celebrating her heroic compassion and "cortesia" and developing in detail the psychological struggle between the desire for revenge and the compassion which she endures. The Italian story is almost pagan in tone. The mother begs her adopted son to keep her memory alive following her death, and the teller's final words are a description of the marble tomb on which engraved verses bear witness to the mother's "cortesia" to future generations. The one Christian implication of the story is contained in the mother's description of her inner struggle as a trial sent by God. In Giraldi's tale the slayer is a secondary figure. Unlike Banedre he is not making a quest which demands sin, self-knowledge, and expiation. A friend of his victim, he lives in the city and is adopted by the mother following the crime. Far from presenting his slaying of the son as a sin, Giraldi claims that it is an accident and directs all moral culpability to the object of the quarrel, a lustful woman. Significantly there are no spatial circumstances accompanying the murder, flight, and refuge in the Italian version. We do not know if the murder occurs at night or day, Scipione is not lost in a foreign city, and nothing is said of his hiding place other than that it is in a house ("luogo ove si pensò che devesse esser sicuro"). Thus the archetypal *Leitmotive* sustaining Cervantes' symbolism—darkness, the labyrinth, the distant light, and enclosing space—are absent in the Italian source. Moreover, the victim of the slayer, who in Cervantes' version represents the bestial condition to which Banedre falls, is in Giraldi's version an ideal son ("tutto gentile e cortese").

One of the most interesting of the southern episodes is the tale of the Scottish countess Ruperta; for it shows how in its eclecticism the *Persiles* can assimilate matter that is entirely chivalric[15] to its underlying theme of the Christian myth of fall and restoration. The countess' husband Lamberto is treacherously slain by a knight whom she has scorned, and the beautiful widow vows to avenge his murder. She clothes herself in black, darkens all her rooms, renounces all bonds with other human beings, surrounds herself with the grisly relics on which she has taken her vow—the skull of her husband, his bloodied shirt, and the stained sword of the assassin—and sets out for Rome to seek the aid of Italian princes in her plan of revenge.

In Ruperta's decision to endure the "trabajos" of her journey to Rome, we observe the perversion of the Christian quest on which the protagonists have embarked. Her relics are demonic equivalents of the Christian symbols which appear repeatedly in the adventures of Periandro and Auristela—the cross, the altar, the Host, and the garments of martyrs and Christians whose afflictions have been healed by Christ and the Virgin. As a victim of desire, she joins many of the other figures of the *Persiles*, who are driven by the illusory desires of the earthly life as they move toward the center at which all desire ends, God. She admits: ". . . en tanto que no llegare a efeto este mi justo, *si no cristiano deseo*,[16] juro que mi vestido será

---

[15] For the numerous echoes from chivalric literature that sound throughout this episode, see María Rosa Lida de Malkiel, "Dos huellas del *Esplandián* en el *Quijote* y el *Persiles*," *Romance Philology*, 9 (1955), 156-162.

[16] The italics are mine.

negro" (p. 386). As if Ruperta's own words and deeds
were not sufficient to present her quest as a surrender to a
morbid passion, at this point the narrator enters with a
learned digression on the physiological causes of anger
and vengeance, announces that Ruperta's intended victim,
Claudio Rubicón, is already dead and that she nevertheless
persists in her desire, seeking the death of his son, and
concludes that the "cólera de la mujer no tiene límite"
(p. 386). As we have already been informed that the son
of the offender is a "gentilhombre en estremo, y de mejores
condiciones que el padre" (p. 385), the introductory appearance of Ruperta in the romance as wronged countess
has completely disintegrated, and she appears now as a
bloodthirsty creature driven by an insane passion. This
impression is heightened as Cervantes immediately describes her contemplating her relics and swearing with
rage: "parecía que arrojaba por los ojos, no lágrimas, sino
fuego, y por la boca, no suspiros, sino humo" (p. 387).

What we observe in these words is the introduction
through allusion of the familiar chivalric theme of the
dragon. In the normal situation of the romance of chivalry
the treacherous Claudino Rubicón would be identified
with the evil forces which devastate the kingdom of the
widowed queen. As in so many of the other episodes,
Cervantes wishes to present the cycle of catastrophe and
restoration in terms of the Christian ethical pattern of sin,
self-knowledge, and redemption. Hence he presents the
heroine as a victim of wrath and, preserving the chivalric
background of the episode, transforms her into the force
that scourges the kingdom. In other words, in her anger
Ruperta descends to the level of the demonic beast, and as
such she is linked in the total context of the *Persiles* with

the hungry wolves to which Antonio is drawn, the wolf-witch whose lascivious advances Rutilio must endure, the ship-leviathan, the apes of the island paradise, and the serpent of Feliciana's song.

Moreover, in the "fire and smoke" of the beautiful dragon, we observe once again the motif of fire, both as the purgatorial fires through which the elect must pass and as an instrument of destruction in the hands of divine and demonic powers. Like the reference to Hercules' shirt in the adventure of Domicio, the brief allusion is sufficient to recreate in the episode all the major fires of the *Persiles* —those of the island of the barbarians, Policarpo's palace, the church in Valencia, and the kitchen of the inn in France. The traditional sterility menacing the queen and her land in the romance of chivalry is emblematically presented in Ruperta's relics (as one of her "insignias dolorosas," her husband's skull is described as a "cabeza sin lengua") and in her surrogate husband, an aged squire who dresses in black and acts as custodian of the relics. The darkness of her dress, her rooms, and her servants' clothes and her self-imposed isolation are the familiar motifs of "near-death" and sterility which we observe in nearly all the moments of descent in the recurrent cycle. The association of Ruperta with demonic forces, implicit in the dragon allusion, is reinforced by the description of her servant as "una sombra negra" (p. 387).

In terms of the Christian cycle of sin and redemption, Ruperta must confront and overcome her sin; in terms of the chivalric pattern which Cervantes has introduced, the dragon must be slain, fertility restored to the land, and the queen married by the redeemer. Both patterns are fulfilled in the climactic bedroom scene. Holding in her hand a knife, "instrumento del cruel sacrificio," Ruperta, "sepultada en maravilloso silencio," approaches the bed of her intended victim and opens the shutter of her lantern. The introduction of light announces the turn of the cycle and the moment of restoration. Indeed what has up to this point been a prolonged and dense orchestration of motifs of darkness (black dress, darkened room, night) suddenly turns into a triumphant statement of motifs of light. Ruperta unexpectedly discovers on the bed of her intended victim the abomination of her act and at the same time her redeemer, who, in keeping with the underlying chivalric pattern, appears as the sun dispelling the clouds of night.

> . . . descubrió el rostro de Croriano . . . halló tanta hermosura, que fue bastante a hacerle caer el cuchillo de la mano, y a que diese lugar la consideración del inorme caso que cometer quería; vio que la belleza de Croriano, como hace el sol a la niebla, ahuyentaba las sombras de la muerte que darle quería, y en un instante no le escogió para víctima del cruel sacrificio, sino para holocausto santo de su gusto.   (p. 389)

In the midst of this synthesis of elements from pagan romance and orthodox Christianity, Cervantes turns to the realm of classical myth to enrich the texture of the scene and reinforce the underlying pattern of fall and rebirth. In the confusion that accompanies her repentance, Ruperta accidentally drops her lantern on the chest of her slumbering Cupid, exposing herself to a final moment of danger and darkness. As is generally the case in the *Persiles*, the myth is thematically relevant, associating the "trabajos" and salvation of Ruperta with the ordeals which Psyche must suffer and overcome to be reborn as goddess and reunited with her beautiful lover, Cupid. Once again darkness and potential disaster give way to light and salvation, as Croriano's servants enter with torches and the young man discovers "la bellísima viuda, como quien ve a la resplandeciente luna de nubes blancas rodeada." In the pattern of darkness-light motifs within the episode and the entire *Persiles*, the transformation of the somber Ruperta into the moon is symbolic of her moral regeneration and parallels the description of her redeemer, Croriano, as the sun. Thus the "solar" hero arrives to save the heroine, the demonic flames of the dragon are transmuted into the "holy holocaust" of pleasure, and the triumphant marriage immediately follows. A series of antitheses celebrating the cyclical movement toward restoration in the familiar series of preterites concludes the adventure: "Triunfó aquella noche la blanda paz desta dura guerra; volvióse el campo de la batalla en tálamo de desposorio; nació la paz de la ira; de la muerte, la vida; y del disgusto, el contento. Amaneció el día, y halló a los recién desposados cada uno en los brazos del otro" (p. 391).

A mood of festivity, typical of comedy, accompanies the denouement of the adventure of Ruperta. On the following morning, the pilgrims joyfully enter the bedroom to congratulate the wedded couple and watch, as the one dissenter amid the joy is banished from the stage. The exit of the ancient squire with the grisly relics is certainly symbolic of Ruperta's achievement of self-knowledge, the overthrow of the dragon, and the restoration of fertility, all of which have been brought about in the nocturnal encounter. However, Cervantes adds a note of humor to his departure, lightening the weight of the seriousness that surrounds this figure in his symbolic role by suddenly allowing him to appear as a human being. He alone protests against what is clearly the happy and the natural solution to the misfortunes of the beautiful widow. In his senile mutterings about the inconstancy of women, which implicitly defend the outrageous law of revenge by which Ruperta was acting, the "minister of death" suddenly appears in a new perspective, in which he is far less sinister than ridiculous.

Like the other episodes the story of Ruperta reenacts the cycle of fall and ascent which forms the thematic and structural basis of the main plot, and like that of the main plot the narrative begins at a low point in the cycle and moves backward, illuminating the original fall, and forward toward the restoration. What should be noted in the resolution of this episode is the increasing movement toward comedy in the second half of the *Persiles*. As has been pointed out above, the movement begins in the scene of festivity in which the inhabitants of Lisbon celebrate the arrival of the pilgrims from the north. Here Cervantes goes further, adding to the note of universal festivity the note of humor. Again it must be recalled that in the second half of the *Persiles* the dominating turn of the tragicomic cycle of human life according to the Christian myth is that of ascent, restoration, and comedy.

Three other episodes present the whole cycle of "los trabajos" in a humorous context, and they can be seen as playful restatements of the major theme of the *Persiles*. In each case Cervantes' mastery of the art of the *entremés* is evident, as humor springs from the lively exchange of dialogue and comedy of situation. In the interlude of the counterfeit captives Cervantes describes the performance of two itinerant showmen who travel through the villages

of Spain disguised as captives, recite a tale of their sufferings in Algiers, display a portable canvas depicting their
adventures, and collect a fee from their sympathetic audi-
ences. A humorless magistrate observes that their knowledge of Algiers is rather limited, discovers that they are
in reality students, and condemns them to the galleys.
Elsewhere I have shown how the entire scene is dominated
by literary concerns, as Cervantes uses the encounter between story teller and critical audience to examine the
neoclassical principles underlying the creation of the
Persiles.[17] Here it remains for me to observe that the students endure a "trabajo," as they are threatened with imprisonment and torture and pardoned at the last moment.
Moreover, this episode contains a fictional repetition of
the cycle within the movement of the surrounding cycle.
In the students' feigned "historia" the protagonists are
held in captivity in Algiers, are bloodied by the blows of
their captor, the Turk Dragut, and must strain at the oar
of his ship as it is pursued by four Christian vessels. As it
repeats various of the recurrent motifs of the main plot
in a context of low comedy—the "mazmorra" of Tetuan,
the demonic Turk who persecutes the heroes, and the
"near-death" which they suffer at his hands—the fictional
account represents a playful variation on the major theme
of the work. Although this degree of play with the serious
theme, which approaches parody, is never reached again
in the *Persiles*, there are two other moments when the
tone of comedy dominates in the statement of theme.

As in the episode of the counterfeit captives, in the episode of the festival in Toledo, the figure of the magistrate
represents both the force of an unnatural law menacing

[17] See *Cervantes, Aristotle, and the "Persiles,"* Ch. V.

137

the protagonists, and the opponent of the comic spirit, who is rendered ridiculous in his opposition and subsequently incorporated into the triumphant comic society. The magistrate discovers the young Tozuelo, dressed as a maiden, dancing in his daughter's place in the festival for the king, and threatens him with punishment. It is quickly revealed that the maiden cannot participate for the traditional reason, and, in a rapid exchange of dialogue, the parties involved decide that the secret marriage of the couple should be sanctioned. The brief incident concludes with the resumption of the dances, which celebrate the triumphant restoration of order through marriage.

In the episode of Isabela Castrucho and Andrea Marulo, a more complete development of that of the festival in Toledo, Cervantes assimilates the traditional formula of Greek New Comedy to his underlying pattern of fall and restoration. The young Isabela Castrucho is in love with Andrea, a student of Salamanca, but her desire to marry him is frustrated by the will of her guardian, an aged uncle, who has already chosen a husband for her. In the city of Lucca the resourceful young lady works out an ingenious plan for deceiving her uncle. She feigns madness, claims to be possessed by the devil, and states that in three days the devil will abandon her body when a man named Andrea Marulo, whom her uncle does not know, will arrive from Spain. The young man has been informed of the plan by letter, and appears at the right moment to act out perfectly his part in the scene of deception, rushing into the bedroom and shouting: "¡Afuera, afuera, afuera; aparta, aparta, aparta; que entra el valeroso Andrea, cuadrillero mayor de todo el infierno, si es que no basta de una escuadra!" (p. 409). The two join hands, announce their marriage, and exorcise all "los demonios que quisieren estorbar tan sabroso nudo," while the uncle stands by in bewilderment, incapable of appreciating the humor that rises from his transformation into the devil. Indeed the humor that permeates this episode is based on the introduction of supernatural forces of heaven and hell into the action by the resourceful Isabela and the unquestioning acceptance of the presence of these forces by the humorless society which the young couple must overcome.

In relation to the overall movement of the *Persiles* we observe here a comic restatement of the cycle of bondage and liberation on which the main plot and most of the episodes are based. Isabela passes through the moment of "near-death," as she lies tied to her bed, attempting to eat her own flesh, screaming about the demons within her, and addressing the pilgrims as angels from heaven sent to deliver her, to the moment of deliverance, as the devils are cast out and she marries her beloved. Similarly we discover the imaginative linkage of the events of the comic action to the Christian myth in the familiar symbols and motifs—"ángeles," "demonio," "Satanás," "ligaduras," the "cruz" and "agua bendita," with which the uncle tries to cure the possessed girl, "los Evangelios," which the priests read to the girl, and the movements from death to rebirth and sterility to fertility through marriage ("Paso hambre, porque espero hartura" [p. 407] and ". . . vos sois señora de mi voluntad, descanso de mi trabajo y vida de mi muerte. Dadme la mano de ser mi esposa, señora mía, y sacadme de la esclavitud en que me veo, a la libertad de verme debajo de vuestro yugo"

139

[p. 410]). It should be observed that the humor of this adventure, like that of the counterfeit captives and the festival in Toledo, does not strike at the basic theme of the *Persiles*. Far from being reductive, it is a humor which rises precisely because the foundation of that which suddenly appears in a new perspective as incongruous is so unshakably founded. What we observe here is simply another variation on the major theme, one step further in the modulation toward a festive tonality in the second half of the *Persiles*.

It is significant that Cervantes refuses to allow the tone of comedy to dominate entirely in the conclusion of the episode. The normal comic solution would demand that the aged uncle, the force opposing the fulfillment of the wishes of the young couple and the observers—the pilgrims and the reader—be reconciled to their inevitable triumph and incorporated into their joyful society. As if remembering suddenly that the *Persiles* is the presentation of both moments of the cycle and that the comic solution and light tone of this episode threaten to banish entirely the shadows surrounding the moment of descent, Cervantes has the uncle collapse and die without blessing the union of Andrea and Isabela. The antithetical phrases introduced by the preterite, "Lleváronle sus criados al lecho, levantóse del suyo Isabela" (p. 411), restore the balance between death and rebirth, which has momentarily been upset, and the concluding paragraph rejects the unqualified tone of festivity, which normally celebrates a comic solution, for a tone of awe and humility before the movement of life through its recurrent cycle of birth, marriage, and death. To give the episode this unexpected turn, Cervantes introduces here an infant

140

brother of Andrea, whose baptism coincides with the marriage of Andrea and Isabela and the burial of the uncle.

> . . . entraron por la puerta de una iglesia un niño, hermano de Andrea Marulo, a bautizar; Isabela y Andrea a casarse, y a enterrar el cuerpo de su tío, porque se vean cuán estraños son los sucesos desta vida; unos a un mismo punto se bautizan, otros se casan, y otros se entierran. Con todo eso, se puso luto Isabela, porque ésta que llaman muerte mezcla los tálamos con las sepulturas y las galas con los lutos.
>
> (pp. 411-412)[18]

What we perceive in the discordant elements in the denouement of this delightful *entremés*—the death of the uncle, the appearance of an infant, and the donning of mourning robes by the bride—is the resurgence of a dark undertone, a return of the shadows of the northern world,[19] which, as Cervantes knows, can never be banished entirely from the earthly life of "trabajos."

[18] Such antitheses, which appear throughout the *Persiles* (see above), reflect stylistically the underlying vision of human life according to the cyclical pattern of the Christian myth. The members of the antitheses hold the opposing moments of the cycle (e.g., death-rebirth, darkness-light, etc.) in close interdependency.

[19] The effect of these elements demonstrates well the workings of the *Leitmotiv* (i.e., "Das Leitmotiv lässt in Musik und Dichtkunst Früheres wiederanklingen, um Zusammenhänge gefühlsmässig zu versinnlichen" [Walzel, op. cit., p. 78]). Just as light is always present but distant and dim in the northern adventures, in the southern adventures darkness is always present but distant. The variations of the motif correspond to the overall tonalities of the respective parts.

CONCLUSION: THE STRUCTURE OF THE *PERSILES*:
TWO ANALOGIES

The mysterious words of wisdom which Auristela offers Periandro following her instruction by the penitentiaries in Rome form an appropriate conclusion to the analysis of the structure of the *Persiles*. For the words not only represent a concise statement of the vision which animates the work, but also provide a revealing analogy of its structure.

> Nuestras almas, como tú bien sabes, y como aquí me han enseñado, siempre están en continuo movimiento y no pueden parar sino en Dios, como en su centro. En esta vida los deseos son infinitos, y unos se encadenan de otros, y se eslabonan, y van formando una cadena que tal vez llega al cielo, y tal se sume en el infierno. (pp. 458-459)

Indeed it could be said that just as Periandro here discovers the secret that illuminates all the dark paths on which the quest has borne the heroes, so the reader finds in Auristela's words a key which enables him to move through the narrative labyrinth which the surface of the *Persiles* represents and comprehend the aesthetic coherence of the work. The key lies in the implications of the metaphor of the "cadena."

On the one hand, the archetypal chain linking the earthly and supernatural realms is a conventional vehicle for the description of the vertical movement of the Christian Everyman in his ascent to heaven or his descent to hell. Evoking the archetype, Auristela's chain becomes an apt analogy for the pilgrimage of the heroes from the end of the earth to Rome, the simulacrum of the Heavenly

City, for, as has been pointed out above, at one level of the symbolic meaning contained in the *Persiles,* the pilgrimage represents the salvation of the human soul and its ascent to heaven. On the other hand, the analogy of the chain is well suited to convey the Christian belief that the apparent confusion and aimless movement marking the earthly life and human history moves in a divinely ordained direction and can ultimately be reduced to a simple paradigm. For although the links of a chain may be infinite in number, they are nonetheless identical in form and lead in a fixed direction.

In addition to the obvious implications of the metaphor in relation to the thematic unity of the *Persiles,*[20] the chain, moreover, offers a vivid visual analogy of the structure of the work. The seemingly endless series of adventures in the main plot and the episodes, the independence and completeness of each episode, the cyclical structure of fall and restoration which gives all adventures and episodes the same circular pattern, and the tortuous movement ever forward, ascending from the depths of the dungeon-cave to the hill overlooking Rome, are all structural qualities which can be expressed effectively through metaphorical concentration in the links of a chain extending in a fixed direction.

As effective as the metaphor which Cervantes offers in Auristela's words is in revealing the vision and the structure of the *Persiles,* it remains a spatial analogy and as such fails to render certain effects of the work which depend on the fact that the *Persiles,* as a work of literature,

[20] See Avalle-Arce's discussion of the idea of the "great chain of being" in the romance ("Introduction" to his edition of the *Persiles* [Madrid, 1969], pp. 20-22).

is apprehended in time.[21] These effects are rapid move-ment, recurrence, confusing accumulation, and powerful repose when confusion yields to order. To discuss such effects in relation to qualities within the work, I think that it is useful to employ an analogy derived from an artistic medium which like literature can exist only in the tem-poral dimension—music.[22] In passing, it is worth recalling here that Friedrich Schlegel enthusiastically judged the *Galatea, Don Quixote,* and the *Persiles* to be *musical* in style.[23] Although Schlegel's observation is anything but clear as it stands and remains an undeveloped intui-

---

[21] To avoid a possible confusion, I should point out that tem-porality in my present context, i.e., in reference to the duration of the reader's apprehension in reading a work, is in no way related to temporality as a thematic ingredient of the work. Above I pointed out that temporality, a basic theme of novelistic literature, is absent in the *Persiles*.

[22] In introducing the analogy of the fugue, as well as such terms as *motif, tonality,* and *movement,* I have no intention of suggesting that Cervantes imitated a musical form (which incidentally was only in its incipient stages of development during his lifetime), just as a critic of modern poetry has no intention of claiming that in the images of an expressionistic poem a poet necessarily imitated a style of painting. I am simply using the terminology of two artistic media, which are in one sense exclusively temporal—they must be apprehended as a *succession* or *movement* of phenomena in time—to discuss in a meaningful way effects which depend on their temporality.

[23] *Wissenschaft der Europäischen Literatur, Kritische Ausgabe* (Zürich, 1958) 11, 160. Arturo Farinelli resorts to musical ter-minology to describe his impressions on reading the *Persiles*: "Sin-fonía más que novela; acorde armónico de mil y mil voces distintas que cantan su música de la vida" (op. cit., p. 115). Hatzfeld has applied the principle of musical motif to the *Quixote* (op. cit., Ch. I).

tion in his work, it suggests, I think, a rewarding way of approaching the problem of the structure of the *Persiles*. In my analysis of the cyclical movement in the adventures of the protagonists and the characters whom they meet, I have often used the general musical terms, *motif, tonality, movement,* and *modulation* and occasionally drawn parallels between the structure of the *Persiles* and fugal composition. In conclusion to my analysis I wish to return to the structural analogy of the fugue.

Far from achieving that linear unity which the sixteenth-century Aristotelians celebrated in the works of Virgil and Heliodorus, the *Persiles* presents a richly interwoven texture, the coherence of which can be compared to that of the contrapuntal web of a fugue. The sudden shifts from main plot to an episode which analogically reenacts it, the rapid conclusion of episodes and immediate introduction of others, the maintenance of the various narrative threads simultaneously (the fragmentary expository technique of Heliodorus is developed to new expressive powers), the sudden intersection of main plot and episode, are all narrative techniques analogous to the ways in which the composer of a fugue develops contrapuntally the episodic variation of the main subject, allowing its entry simultaneously with one and another episode.

Like that of a fugue, the power of the *Persiles* is based on the principles of fragmentation, recurrence, and accumulation in the seemingly endless repetition and variation of a basic theme which is announced most clearly in the opening scene. Corresponding to the fugal polarization of the basic theme into subject and answer is the complex of antithetical motifs accompanying the two moments of the cyclical pattern which the *Persiles* celebrates: bondage-liberation, despair-triumphant vision, death-rebirth, darkness-light, menacing space-the temple, the wilderness-the city, sterility-fertility, fear-hope, isolation-marriage, and confusion-harmony.

The effect of such fragmentation and repetition in the *Persiles* is, I think, similar to that of the fugal recurrence of motifs. Repeating the past and prefiguring the future, each major moment of the narrative acquires something of the intensity characteristic of the heightened moment of the mystic. The work thus achieves a type of sequential or temporal monumentality. Moreover, like a fugue the *Persiles* moves not toward the overcoming of one of the polarities by the other, but rather toward a resolution in which both are maintained in a higher synthesis, which is dependent on their opposition. A final tonality is reached, and one of the motif-clusters dominates, but the other remains implicitly present.[24] The effect of a recon-

---

[24] Herman Nohl observes that music is the artistic medium which, by virtue of its capacity to develop simultaneously opposing moods, most effectively presents such a higher synthesis of opposites ("das Moment der Gegensätzlichkeit und ihrer Einheit"). "Wie bei Hegel in jedem Satz die Einschränkung, die Antithese mit dazu gehört, das Ja und das Aber, das nicht draussen bleibt, sondern mit seiner positiven Beziehung auf das Ja erst das Ganze ausmacht. . . . Vor allem ist aber die Musik imstande, diese rätselhafte Einheit der Gegensätze in einer Harmonie auszusprechen, gerade aus den grausamsten Dissonanzen die höchste Versöhnung zu schöpfen. Auch hier ist Bach wieder das grossartigste Beispiel, wenn er in seinen Doppelfugen das Gegeneinander der Gemütsstimmungen sich ausarbeiten lässt, in seinen Kantaten Sündenbewusstsein, Erlösungshoffnung und befreite Seligkeit gleichzeitig zusammenklingen" (*Stil und Weltanschauung* [Jena, 1920], p. 113).

ciliation of opposites derives from the endless recurrence of *both* moments of the cycle and from the frequent antitheses which reinforce the close interdependency of the moments. It is most forcefully produced, however, when the dominance of the triumphant moment of the cycle is unexpectedly countered by the emergence of one of the motifs accompanying the lower moment. Such are Arnaldo's report, late in the romance, that the barbarians have risen from the ashes of their northern kingdom and reinstituted their repugnant customs; the death of the uncle, which clothes the bride Isabela in mourning; the death of the count following his marriage to Antonio's daughter; and, what is equally striking, Cervantes' reference to the continuing sinfulness of Bartolomé and Luisa amid the celebration of the various marriages and their fruits at the conclusion of the work.

Just as the fugal web leads through a plan of modulations to the climactic restatement of the subject, the *Persiles* modulates from a dark tonality in the first half, whose dominant motifs are bondage, death, darkness, and the light which shines dimly in the distance, to a light tonality in the second, whose dominant motifs are liberation, rebirth, light, and darkness overcome. As the tone of festivity increases, Cervantes occasionally can, like the composer of fugue in his multiple variations, play with his major subject, introducing the note of triumphant parody into the work.[25] The movement of the fugue is through the maze of counterpoint toward a clear, triumphant statement of its subject, the climactic moment at

[25] He does so in the episodes of the counterfeit captives, the festival in Toledo, and the wedding of Isabel Castrucho (see above, pp. 136-141).

which the wanderings of the subject are rewarded with long-awaited repose that is solemnized in the massive blocks of harmony of the coda. Structurally and thematically the *Persiles* moves toward such a moment, the arrival at Rome, where all the narrative threads of the work are caught up and unraveled and where the pilgrims discover the image of that point at which all desire ends and toward which the pilgrimage of Everyman on the tortuous paths of the earthly life leads.

CHAPTER FOUR

Literature in the *Quixote* and the *Persiles*

A TALE of life overcoming death, of music calming tempests, a tale almost childlike in its thematic simplicity and repetitions. A dim landscape where dreams of gardens and song banish nightmare visions of destruction and death, and distant stars bear witness from above that the guiding hand of Providence is ever present amid life's sorrows. How like a fairy tale, we might say. And how unlikely in the writer whose major work freed man from the shackles of transcendentalism and its literary paradigms, creating the genre which has been called the literary offspring of mature humanity.[1]

The fact is that the *Persiles* and the *Quixote* are about as different as two works of literature could possibly be. In the *Quixote* Cervantes reminds us that the poetic justice which governs the world of fairy tales is sadly lacking in actuality, that human experience is irreducible and infinite in its variety, nuances, and gradations, and that it is most valuable precisely because of its irreducibility. In the *Persiles* he prefers to strip away all such gradations and affirm that beneath their teeming surface there is in fact a fundamental pattern which gives life a uniform shape and that there are clear-cut truths which man can rely on. The ambiguities of experience which fascinated Cervantes from the first paragraph of the *Quixote* to its conclusion are nowhere to be found in the *Persiles*. The darkness-light and death-life contrasts of its opening paragraph introduce a work founded on a series of carefully

[1] See Georg Lukács, *Die Theorie des Romans* (Berlin, 1920).

organized antitheses, which are formulated in a context of metaphysical and ethical abstractions and are resolved with absolute clarity. The *Quixote* is also built on antitheses, but they appear in the gray area of existential problems, and their tension is more often than not left unresolved.

In conceiving the *Persiles* Cervantes stood back from the surface of life, and in his lengthened perspective he saw that man's essential nature is moral and that the essential nature of life lies in its rhythm of birth-death-salvation.[2] In the genre of romance he discovered literary conventions well suited to the expression of his vision— a concentration on simple schemes of value and simple polarizations of emotion, a disdain for existential ambiguities, and, most important, a cyclical movement from destruction through peripeteias and recognitions to resurrection, a movement which reflects powerfully the fundamental rhythm of life.

It is idle to insist on seeing Cervantes' turn to romance as a renunciation of the *Quixote*, his "anti-romance," and to speculate about biographical reasons for the differences between the works. While it is true that Cervantes asserted that there are times when one dare not take the next life in jest, it is also true that his fascination with the uncertainties of the earthly life continued unabated while he planned and wrote the *Persiles*. Although the final book was not completed until shortly before Cervantes' death, the writing of much of the work was simultaneous

[2] "El *Persiles* será la aventura del propio Cervantes, pues, habiendo cortado las amarras que lo atan al relativismo humano, hace rumbo hacia los inexplorados mares del Universal Absoluto" (Avalle-Arce, *Deslindes Cervantinos* [Madrid, 1961], p. 73).

with that of the *Quixote*. The differences between the *Persiles* and the *Quixote* should be viewed rather as the differences between two literary genres, each with its own laws and each particularly adjusted to a certain vision or statement about life. Cervantes is not alone among great artists in his capacity to cultivate radically different genres and embrace seemingly contradictory visions of life.

While the important role of literature in the *Quixote* has always been recognized, little attention has been given to its significance in the *Persiles*. The statements of the two works about the function of literature are as different as their respective conclusions concerning existence and morality. Everywhere in the *Quixote* we observe a process which Harry Levin aptly summarizes thus: "Through its many varieties of two-sided observation, there runs a single pattern: the pattern of art embarrassed by confrontation with nature."[3] Although the process is visible every time a literary gesture of the hero is ignored or countered by prosaic reality, it is most interesting in the various scenes in Part One in which Cervantes addresses himself to specific literary forms. The world of the pastoral romance is shattered by a real woman's application of the logic of the "disdainful shepherdess" of literature, by a suicide, and by the ignorance of real goatherds. In the *Curioso impertinente* the ubiquitous romantic tale of the *Two Friends* is somehow embarrassed by what happens between the very best of friends in real life. As Ginés de Pasamonte discusses the qualities of his autobiography with Don Quixote, the negative idealization of picaresque romance is suddenly disturbed by the observation that

[3] "The Example of Cervantes," *Contexts of Criticism* (Cambridge, Mass., 1957), p. 79.

151

galleys and prisons are very unpleasant facts of life and that a profound human problem underlies society's codes of law and justice.

Of the numerous cases in which life's complications arise to mock art's simplifications, one is particularly relevant, as it leads us to the fundamental differences between the *Quixote* and the *Persiles* in their uses of literature. The *Tale of the Captive* is one of the most puzzling episodes in the *Quixote* because in it the pattern of literary romance is thoroughly developed and threatens to collide with and deform the real world, which is otherwise triumphant in the work. In fact, if Cervantes had not developed the figure of Hadji Morato as he did, the tale could be inserted in the *Persiles* and read as one more re-actualization of the Christian mythology which the work celebrates. Here we observe a beautiful Christian heroine who, together with her beloved, is delivered from bondage in a demonic lower world and led through a series of harrowing adventures, reversals of fortune, and unexpected recognitions to salvation and marriage in Spain. The narrator makes no secret of the fact that Divine Providence is at work in the ordeals of the fugitive lovers, and, when they arrive at the inn, she mounted on an ass, he at her side, and are told that no room is available, we can see how close Cervantes is to the allegorical methods of the *Persiles*. However, the episode contains something quite unlike anything in the *Persiles*. Between black and white, between the Turks, associated with Satan, and Zoraida, associated with the Virgin, Cervantes interposes the gray realm of human experience. If Cervantes had written this episode for the *Persiles*, Hadji Morato, who assumes the role of the chief blocking agent in the pattern of romance, would have taken his place beside the other diabolical agents who attempt to thwart the designs of the heroes. We need only look at the episode of the *Persiles* most similar to the *Tale of the Captive*, the betrayal of the coastal village by the *moriscos*, and to the sinister figure of Rafala's father to discover how the character Hadji Morato would have emerged in the romance. However, Cervantes endows this man with such characteristics as fatherly love, courtesy, and kindness, and allows him to move briefly in a situation of ordinary life. The result is a humanization of the figure and a sudden disruption of the developing romantic situation. The naive morality[4] which we demand in romance vanishes, and the convenient polarization of emotion which we experience in reading romances is no longer possible, for beside the ambiguities of the human condition suggested by the pathos of Hadji Morato as his daughter abandons him, the realization of the fairy-tale pattern and the impressive achievement of Divine Providence strike us as somehow irrelevant. It might be argued that the *Tale of the Captive* is puzzling because Cervantes has unsatisfactorily combined the techniques of two different literary genres, romance and novel, in the presentation of character. Such a position, however, overlooks the fact that the peculiar mixture is consistent with the essential proc-

[4] I borrow the term from André Jolles' discussion of the fairy tale (*Einfache Formen* [Tübingen, 1930], pp. 240-241). Such a morality is founded not on principles of conduct but rather on our judgment of "the way things ought to turn out in the world." It is independent of specific religions and has nothing to do with utility. It is the type of morality we have in mind when we speak of "poetic justice."

ess of the *Quixote* (particularly in Part One) of exposing the violence which literature does to life.[5]

If in the *Quixote* Cervantes depicts life repeatedly shattering the mirror of art, in the *Persiles* he reconstructs the mirror, and the result is a work of widely ranging tonalities and immense literary variety. The reach of the echoes, styles, and genres which it assimilates extends from the contemporary comedy, farce, and religious and courtly drama, the Italian novella, and the lyric poem back to medieval and classical romance, the classical epic, and the Bible and holy legends. Its conceptual texture varies from the density of pure allegory to the transparency of pure adventure. Its tonalities range from the lyrical beauty of Feliciana's hymn to the Virgin to the dark humor of Bartolomé's "picaresque" epistle, from the iconic brilliance of the island masque to the farcical atmosphere of the counterfeit captive's recitation, and from the canonical solemnity of Antonio's cave, which recalls the *autos sacramentales*, to the festivity of Isabel Castrucho's bedroom and the melodramatic sensationalism of Feliciana's

---

[5] I have chosen to emphasize the literary implications of the episode. As Spitzer has argued, in its ethical and metaphysical implications the scene can be read as an indictment of the whimsicality of Divine Providence (see "Linguistic Perspectivism in the *Don Quijote*," *Linguistics and Literary History* [New York, 1962], pp. 65-68). When Cervantes alludes to *Cava Rumia*, he employs the allegorical methods characteristic of romance to disjoint the romance pattern and reinforce the ambiguity arising from Hadji Morato's humanity. Is Zoraida an analogue of the Virgin or of La Cava, the legendary evil woman who caused the loss of Spain? The ethical and literary dimensions of the episode are perfectly consistent with one another, as the liberation of man from literary paradigms presupposes his liberation from transcendental schemes.

flight before her vengeful father. Moreover, the characters of the *Persiles* are highly conscious of literature, associating their actions with literary analogues, slipping well-known verses of Garcilaso's poetry into their speech, or molding their conversation to fit the complex patterns of contemporary poetic and rhetorical discourse. Indeed, the process which Vossler and Spitzer have studied in Lope's *Dorotea* and described as the "Literarisierung des Lebens" is often visible in the *Persiles*. However, unlike the *Dorotea*, which concludes in the somber tonality of the morality play, the *Persiles* never regards literature as a vanity or a temptation. And unlike the *Quixote*, it has no interest in measuring the unrealities of literary content by the realities of experience or the literary "deformations" of language by the style of ordinary discourse.

If Cervantes tells us in *Quixote* that, in its lack of sophistication, idealizing literature is of little use to the artist who would attempt to grasp the multiple ambiguities of man in temporality, in the *Persiles* he seems to affirm that the varied forms of such literature are founded on the essential rhythm of life, the cycle of death and birth, and have evolved in close kinship with the religious rituals and myths by which man celebrates that rhythm. Examined in this light, the transfigurations of life by literature become not deformations but rather distillations of essential realities which are rarely visible in the confusion of existential phenomena.

In the *Quixote* Cervantes frees literature from its bondage in literature and points to the major path which it was to follow from the eighteenth century to the present. In the *Persiles* he turns about to create a mosaic of literary reminiscences, embracing the multiple forms and styles of literature to heighten the spectacular effect of his final celebration of the Christian vision of man and history. We might explain the function of literature in the *Persiles* as Cervantes' homage to neoclassical precepts concerning the imitation of models or as one more example of the literary eclecticism characteristic of baroque literature. However, its full significance can be recognized only if we bear in mind the antagonisms between life and literature and myth everywhere evident in the *Quixote*. Creating literature from literature, Cervantes affirms in the *Persiles* the age-old kinship between myth, religion, and literature and between the artist and the myth-maker. Reversing his position in the *Quixote*, where the poet appears as a protean figure who delights in presenting unresolved contradictions and existential dilemmas and in exposing the poverty of any system which lays claim to absolute reliability, the Cervantes of the *Persiles* stands firm in the Renaissance neoclassicists' faith in the poet as the descendant of Orpheus, the builder of civilization, educator of humanity, and revealer of divine truth. Shakespeare wrote that Orpheus' song could "Make tigers tame and huge leviathans/ Forsake unsounded deeps to dance on sands." To borrow the mythological vocabulary of the Renaissance, we might say that Cervantes concludes his career as a writer by taking up the lyre of Orpheus.

EPILOGUE

The Poet's Farewell
Where Life and Literature Meet

O N CONCLUDING the *Persiles*, Cervantes was aware that
his death was approaching and began his dedication
to the Count of Lemos by recalling an ancient song:

> "Puesto ya el pie en el estribo,
> Con las ansias de la muerte,
> Gran señor, ésta te escribo."

On perhaps the same day, Tuesday, April 19, 1616, he
penned a prologue to the *Persiles*, in which he describes an
encounter with a youthful admirer on the road to Madrid,
announces that he will die on or before the following
Sunday, and bids his friends farewell.

The autobiographical anecdote is curious and has been
by and large ignored by Cervantine scholarship.[1] I find
the prologue most interesting because, in offering Cervantes' final commentary on himself and the earthly life,
it employs two of the most persistent symbols not only of
the work which it introduces, but also of Cervantes' entire
literary production—the open road and the city. Indeed
the anecdote ends where so many of Cervantes' tales end:
the protagonist emerges from the open spaces in which
he has wandered to enter the city or the house, the symbol

---

[1] An exception is the allegorical reading of Singleton, who observes in it a veiled apology for the inferiority of the work which
it introduces (see "El misterio del *Persiles*," *Realidad*, 2 [1947],
237-253).

of social order and ultimately the symbol of the divine order—the City or House of God.[2]

It should be recalled here that triumphant return, the theme of the *Persiles,* the *Gitanilla,* the *Tale of the Captive,* and several of Cervantes' other works, does not always dominate in Cervantes' writings. In the *Quixote* the house is obviously the symbol of the social order to which the

[2] Leo Spitzer's words describe Cervantes' tales of triumphant return very well: "Christentum und Familie sind Eines: das den Menschen Umfassende, Bettende und Hegende, von dem man sich nur loslöst, um desto gläubiger zurückzukehren" ("Die Frage der Heuchelei des Cervantes," *Zeitschrift für Romanische Philologie,* 56 [1936], 165). Although my interpretations of the symbols of the city and the open road are based entirely on the patterns I have observed in Cervantes' works and occasionally in the literary tradition which nourished them, it is useful, I think, to point out how certain other methods of interpretation might support my conclusions as to what perhaps Cervantes' last written words signified. In his psychological studies, Jung observes in the path of wandering and the city two of the many images or archetypes through which the unconscious creative force, the libido, manifests itself universally. ". . . wandering is a symbol of longing, of the restless urge which never finds its object, of nostalgia for the lost mother" (*Symbols of Transformation,* tr. R.F.C. Hull, Bollingen Series XX: 5 [Princeton, 1967], I, p. 205). "The city is a maternal symbol, a woman who harbours the inhabitants in herself like children" [e.g., the Heavenly City of the Revelation appears as a bride; Rome and her Church appear as a mother] (p. 208). In these terms Cervantes' entry into the city could be interpreted psychologically as his own serene departure from that world of unfulfilled desire, in which his characters are tossed about, to find the long awaited repose at the bosom of the mother, here symbolized by the city-church. At the same time, Otto Bollnow's phenomenological study of space suggests that the organized, meaningful space of the house and the city, the two recurrent points of return in Cervantes' works, is viewed by man as the point of order amid the chaos of phenom-

knight must return; but in the context of the work its value is ambiguous. It is not only associated with the death of the imagination and the prosaic existence of the bourgeoisie (e.g., the house of the Caballero del Verde Gabán, who is disturbed by his son's desire to be a poet and whose threshold is barricaded against the disruptive forces represented by the books of chivalry; and the house of Alonso Quijana, whose library is condemned and destroyed as a threat to the stability of the house). It is, moreover, the militant cause of those few people in the *Quixote* whom the author judges negatively: the Castilian who destroys the mood of festivity surrounding Don Quixote's triumphant passage through the streets of Barcelona, shouting: "Vuélvete, mentecato, a tu casa, y mira por tu hacienda" (II, 991), and the ecclesiastic who reprimands the Duke for humoring Don Quixote, addressing the latter as "alma de cántaro" and ordering him: "volveos a vuestra casa . . . y curad de vuestra hacienda" (II, 769).

To understand the ambiguity surrounding the victory of the house in *Don Quixote*, we must recall the implications of the unsocial behavior which Cervantes enjoys depicting throughout the work. When the translator of Cide Hamete Benengeli's chronicle edits out a lengthy description of Diego de Miranda's house as irrelevant, Cer-

---

ena that the human being experiences as he exists in time and space (see *Mensch und Raum* [Stuttgart, 1963], pp. 128-129 and p. 145). Opposing this is that unfamiliar space lying beyond their limits (*die Fremde*), into which man is occasionally thrown and in which he finds himself to be a homeless wanderer, seeking always to return to his home within the familiar horizons, which are both spatial and spiritual (ibid., pp. 91-92). In these terms too it is significant that Cervantes' final gesture is a return from the *Fremde* to the city-house which he bore within him, Spain and God.

vantes is indirectly informing us that the most interesting dimensions of human beings are displayed when they depart from the roles offered to them in the standard forms of their culture. As Castro has pointed out, the memorable characters of the *Quixote* are those who dare "to step out of their houses" and create from within themselves an authentic existence.[3] The list ranges from Don Quixote and Sancho to such fleeting but unforgettable figures as Diego de la Llana's daughter, the youthful soldier, and Doña Rodríguez. If we admit that such minor figures are all touched with the madness of the protagonist, then we may say that in the *Quixote* madness is synonymous with the inexhaustible vitality of human nature as it presses for self-expression in ways which may occasionally conflict with all conventionally accepted patterns of behavior. While there is little in the *Quixote*'s fondness for the "open road" that could be construed as heterodox or subversive, its author's lack of interest in a rigid system of values such as that which animates the *Persiles* and its quintessential figures is obvious.[4]

[3] See "La estructura del *Quijote*," *Hacia Cervantes* (Madrid, 1957).

[4] It should be emphasized that the open road of the *Quixote*, unlike that of the *Persiles* extending from Thule to Rome, has no fixed direction. Proceeding from a village in the Mancha whose name the narrator "does not wish to recall," Don Quixote and Sancho ". . . se pusieron a caminar por donde la voluntad de Rocinante quiso, que se llevaba tras sí la de su amo" (I, 196). Despite the return of the protagonists, the *Quixote* is about people on a road whose only direction is personal freedom, that is, away from the molding influences of the city and the house. "La ruta del caballero manchego no es producto de su demencia, sino de la necesidad de mantenerse siendo él quien ha decidido ser,—'yo sé

The novelist then delights in human activity which, when measured by society's standards of value, is at best irrelevant, at worst criminal. Hence it is not surprising to discover throughout Cervantes' writings the association of the artist with exile, distant lands, wandering, criminality, or, in short, with everything to which the city is opposed. In the *Gitanilla* only the poet Clemente is excluded from the festive group which returns to the city, and his exile and descent to criminality are connected with his mission as poet. Moreover, Cervantes' most powerful figure of the artist, Pedro de Urdemalas, boasts of having no home, associates himself with the distant (both the distant of real geography and of the realm of fantasy), claims to possess Proteus' powers of metamorphosis, and suggests that the entire sublunary world is a place of exile over which he as artist is god. Like Don Quixote's antagonists, the opponents of the triumphant artist identify with the house. The practical Inés scolds Belica, Pedro's protégée, who dreams of being a princess, with the words: "¡Acomodaos, noramala,/ a la cocina y la sala . . . !"[5] It

---

quien soy' dirá más tarde. La ruta de don Quijote expresa su estar siendo en él y en Dulcinea: en ella 'tengo vida y ser' [I, 307]. Ni la una ni el otro se prestan a ser trazados geométricamente. Les basta con *ser*" (Castro, *Cervantes y los casticismos españoles*, p. 60).

[5] *Pedro de Urdemalas*, in *Obras completas*, p. 512. In one of the few appearances of the Cervantine figure of the poet in the *Persiles*, his opponent is similarly associated with the house-city. Mauricio, the pedantic critic, expresses his annoyance with Periandro's storytelling by complaining that the youth's fantasies are delaying his return to the city. See *Cervantes, Aristotle, and the "Persiles,"* for a more extensive treatment of these matters, esp. Ch. IX, "The Cervantine Figure of the Poet: Impostor or God?" For the importance of Proteus as a symbol embodying the aims and methods

is hardly necessary to point out the asocial connections of Cide Hamete Benengeli, a magician who descends from a race of liars, is on intimate terms with the devil, and, as a story teller, enjoys mingling truth and falsehood, reality and fiction.

It is clear that Cervantes saw in the open road not only the traditional symbol of the pilgrimage of Everyman in his earthly exile (in the *Persiles*) but also a symbol of all that is irreducible and unique in human experience and all that is unconventional in the artistic mission (in the *Quixote*). His view of the city-house, the symbolic counterweight to the open road, was marked by the same ambivalence—on the one hand, the city as the true home of all Christians and the emblem of Christian values (in the *Persiles*); on the other, the city as culture, a force threatening to impoverish human nature of its protean variety (in the *Quixote*).

To return to the matter at hand, the prologue to the *Persiles* is Cervantes' final comment on himself as a Christian and as a poet. In it he chooses to envision his life as following the path which brings Persiles and Sigismunda and their comrades to Rome, reenacting the ritual which, interpreted allegorically, represents the movement of man through the sublunary world of disorder toward the Heavenly City.[6] As a poet, Cervantes takes his

---

of Renaissance writers, see A. Bartlett Giamatti, "Proteus Unbound: Some Versions of the Sea God in the Renaissance," *The Disciplines of Criticism*, ed. P. Demetz, T. Greene, L. Nelson Jr. (New Haven, Conn., 1968), pp. 437-475.

[6] It is interesting that even in the *Quixote*, an artistic monument to a nontranscendentalist view of man, Cervantes assimilates autobiographical and historical matter to the general vision which ani-

leave of that world, represented in the picturesque figure of the student who overtakes him on the road, pays tribute to him as the "delight of the Muses," and leaves him at the gate of Toledo. Could any symbol express more effectively and delightfully the protean, unsocial aspects of humanity than this energetic youth who struggles unsuccessfully to keep his starched collar straight and sends his bags flying in his eagerness to dismount? Cervantes accepts the homage of the young admirer and requests his company and "buena conversación" for the "little that remains of his journey." At the gate of the city Cervantes bids farewell to the student, embracing him and regretfully uttering the impossible wish to transform him into art. It is an embrace of reconciliation, healing all the antagonisms which may remain between the house and the open road, the Christian and the poet, the *Persiles* and

---

mates the *Persiles*. In *El cautivo* the fall of the Goleta is conceived as a "trabajo" demanded by God ("Pero el cielo lo ordenó de otra manera, no por culpa ni descuido del general que a los nuestros regía, sino por los pecados de la cristiandad, y porque quiere y permite Dios que tengamos siempre verdugos que nos castiguen" [I, 399-400]). Similarly in *El trato de Argel*: Saavedra speaks of his capitivity: "Pero si el alto Cielo en darme enojos/ no está con mi ventura conjurado" (*Obras completas*, p. 117), and his faith that the "trabajo" of the despairing Pedro will be rewarded: ". . . el día llegará, sabroso y dulce,/ do tengas libertad; que el Cielo sabe/ darnos gusto y placer por cien mil vías/ ocultas al humano entendimiento" (p. 141). If we realize that Cervantes could occasionally interpret his life in such symbolic terms and observe in his own experience such "literary" events as the battle with the forces of evil, the victory of the forces of good, bondage in the dungeons of demonic forces, unexpected deliverance, and the perils of the sea, both his creation of the *Persiles* and his valediction at the gate of Madrid become much more meaningful.

the *Quixote*. In his valediction Cervantes expresses to the end his affection for the world of temporality with all its colorful nuances and ambiguities, a world which he is prepared to abandon only when called to the true home of all Christians.

Tornéle a abrazar, volvióseme a ofrecer, picó a su burra, y dejóme tan mal dispuesto como él iba caballero en su burra, a quien había dado gran ocasión a mi pluma para escribir donaires; pero no son todos los tiempos unos. Tiempo vendrá, quizá, donde, anudando este roto hilo, diga lo que aquí me falta, y lo que se convenía. ¡Adiós, gracias; adiós, donaires; adiós, regocijados amigos; que yo me voy muriendo, y deseando veros presto contentos en la otra vida!

(p. 49)

Index

Aesop, 55

Agathon, 9

Amyot, Jacques, 8, 16, 17

Ariosto, Ludovico, 16, 24, 25, 28, 54, 55

Aristotle, 6, 7, 8, 9, 10, 13, 14, 15, 16, 17, 18, 24, 32, 37, 52, 53, 54, 57, 62, 69, 79, 108, 145

Atkinson, William C., 10

Augustine, St., 33

Avalle-Arce, Juan Bautista, 143, 150

Bach, Johann Sebastian, 47, 48, 146

Bataillon, Marcel, 103

Beltrán y Rózpide, Ricardo, 50

Bible, 31, 32, 36, 38, 40, 41, 45, 46, 47, 53, 65, 66, 68, 69, 72, 73, 75, 81, 87, 88, 89, 101, 103, 104, 112, 154

Boccaccio, Giovanni, 11

Boehlich, Walter, 47

Bollnow, Otto F., 44, 158, 159

Bouterwek, Friedrich, 11

Campanella, Tommaso, 28

Canavaggio, Jean-François, 10

Carvallo, Luis Alfonso de, 53, 54

Casalduero, Joaquín, 5, 11, 47, 57, 58, 59, 60, 81

Cascales, Francisco, 14, 121

Castro, Américo, 51, 94, 95, 96, 103, 113, 160, 161

Cervantes Saavedra, Miguel de: *El capitán cautivo*, 15, 152, 153, 158, 163; *El coloquio de los perros*, 52, 114; *El curioso impertinente*, 15, 151; *Don Quijote de la Mancha*, 3, 4, 5, 7, 10, 11, 13, 14, 15, 27, 28, 29, 54, 62, 69, 91, 94, 103, 122, 149ff; *La española inglesa*, 122; *La Galatea*, 4, 14, 22, 91, 144; *La Gitanilla*, 71, 115, 119, 158, 161; *Pedro de Urdemalas*, 161; *El trato de Argel*, 163; *Viaje del Parnaso*, 15

Covarrubias y Orozco, Sebastián de, 32

Croce, Benedetto, 5

Dante Alighieri, 38, 87

D'Audiguier, Vital, 28

De Lollis, Cesare, 4, 5

Dunlap, Rhodes, 53

Eliade, Mircea, 44, 46

Entwistle, William J., 11, 57, 58

Erasmus, Desiderius, 103

Farinelli, Arturo, 4, 7, 35, 144

Fletcher, Angus, 44, 45, 58, 59

Forcione, Alban K., 10, 24, 34, 38, 52, 53, 60, 79, 100, 137, 161

Frye, Northrop, 35, 36, 38, 42, 58, 59, 70, 74, 75, 86

Garcilaso de la Vega, 90, 155

Giamatti, A. Bartlett, 35, 83, 102, 162

Giraldi Cintio, Giovambattista, 14, 130

Hatzfeld, Helmut, 4, 5, 92, 93, 126, 144

Hefti, Victor, 19

Hegel, Georg Wilhelm Friedrich, 146

Heliodorus, 5, 8, 9, 10, 13, 16, 17, 18, 19, 23, 24, 25, 27, 30, 37, 47, 78, 108, 145

Homer, 5, 8, 9, 20, 53, 55, 72, 78

Horace, 6, 13, 14, 100

Jolles, André, 153

Jonson, Ben, 53

Jung, C. G., 158

Kayser, Wolfgang, 65

Krauss, Werner, 29

León, Fray Luis de, 81

Levin, Harry, 151

Lida de Malkiel, María Rosa, 131

López Pinciano, Alonso, 8, 10, 18, 53, 54, 55, 56, 72, 78

Lukács, Georg, 149

Mayáns y Siscar, Gregorio, 28

Menéndez y Pelayo, Marcelino, 4, 5, 12

Minturno, Antonio Sebastiano, 25

Montaigne, Michel de, 53

Montgomery, Robert L. Jr., 54, 56

Nohl, Herman, 48, 146

Osuna, Rafael, 12

Ovid, 52

Pfandl, Ludwig, 72

Pigna, Giovanni Battista, 54

Riley, Edward C., 9, 10, 28, 29, 79

Ríus, Leopoldo, 28

Rohde, Erwin, 19

Romero, Carlos, 10, 121

Rothbauer, Anton, 103, 104

Rousset, Jean, 83

Sánchez, Alberto, 60

Sassetti, Filippo, 25, 27

Savj-López, Paolo, 60

Scaliger, Julius Caesar, 8, 17

Schevill, Rudolph, 3, 28

Schissel von Fleschenberg, Otmar, 19

Schlegel, Friedrich, 144

Shakespeare, William, 156

Shergold, N. D., 83

Singleton, Mack, 4, 157

INDEX

Sismondi, Simonde de, 3
Sosa Coitiño, Manuel de, 65
Spenser, Edmund, 102
Spitzer, Leo, 113, 154, 155, 158
Stegmann, Tilbert Diego, 12
Summo, Faustino, 25

Tasso, Torquato, 6, 7, 8, 9, 10,
  17, 18, 20, 24, 25, 27, 34, 35,
  37, 38, 56, 61, 102, 121
Tatius, Achilles, 8, 19
Toffanin, Giuseppe, 4, 9
Torquemada, Antonio de, 113

Vega, Lope de, 155
Vilanova, Antonio, 9, 32
Virgil, 5, 8, 9, 17, 18, 20, 50,
  52, 71, 72, 78, 101, 102, 145
Vossler, Karl, 155

Wagner, Richard, 47
Walzel, Oskar, 47, 141
Weinberg, Bernard, 25, 28
Willis, Raymond S., 51
Wolff, Samuel, 19

Zimic, Stanislav, 65, 79

PUBLISHED BOOKS IN THIS SERIES

The Orbit of Thomas Mann. By Erich Kahler

On Four Modern Humanists: Hofmannsthal, Gundolf, Curtius, Kantorowicz. Edited by Arthur R. Evans, Jr.

Flaubert and Joyce: The Rite of Fiction. By Richard Cross

A Stage for Poets: Studies in the Theatre of Hugo and Musset. By Charles Affron

Hofmannsthal's Novel *Andreas*. By David Miles

Kazantzakis and the Linguistic Revolution in Greek Literature. By Peter Bien

Modern Greek Writers. Edited by Edmund Keeley and Peter Bien